THE BITCHES OF BEXAR COUNTY

(Pronounced Bear County)

A Memoir

By Pam Moody

Editor: Brenda E. Cortez

Author photo credit: Kamille Donley

Cover Design: Michelle Fairbanks

Interior Layout: Michael Nicloy

ISBN: 979-8-9907205-9-6

Published by: BC Books, LLC
Franklin, Wisconsin
Brenda E. Cortez, Publisher
bcbooksllc.com
Info@bcbooksllc.com

Printed in The United States of America

To my parents, Bob & Charlotte, who gave the word HOME a whole new meaning! Providing me with a life that was beyond AMAZING, passing on their gift of love and laughter while teaching me how NOT to sweat the small stuff.

I can hear Dad saying, "Kill 'em with kindness, kid, it makes people nervous."

I cherish their wisdom and unconditional LOVE!

To Emily, my ONE & ONLY child, my LOVE, my LIGHT, my INSPIRATION, my EVERYTHING!

WITH HEARTS AND HUGS

THE BITCHES OF BEXAR COUNTY

Everyone has a story...

This is mine.

probation *noun*

. the process or period of testing or observing the character or abilities of a person in a certain role.

. the suspending of a convicted offender's sentence during good behavior under the supervision of a probation officer.

. the suspension of all or part of a sentence and its replacement by freedom subject to specific conditions and the supervision of a probation officer.

* also called community supervision

* compare DIVERSION, PAROLE

. probation as a sentence in itself

. the period or state of being subject to probation, probation, from probare to test, approve, prove

probation definition & meaning – Merriam-Webster

probation officer *noun*

. an officer appointed to investigate, report on, and supervise the conduct convicted offenders on probation.

probation officer definition & meaning – Merriam -Webster

a.k.a. protectors of society

cjad/probation Certification Training, Sam Houston State University

(twentieth century)

a.k.a. (current title) agents of change

cjad/community justice assistance division (twenty-first century)

TABLE OF CONTENTS

ACKNOWLEDGEMENTS

In my career as an adult probation officer, I met many people from different walks of life: poor, rich, homeless, old, young, thoughtful and kind, rude and obnoxious. The youngest defendant supervised on my caseload was 17, while the oldest was 93. Most individuals placed under my guidance were polite and compliant, taking the opportunity to better their lives and those of their families. On the other hand, there were some that would challenge me and test my patience to my core. The men and women I have written about are just a few of the people on my caseload. With the permission of some of my colleagues, I have also shared some of their cases.

Some names have been altered or changed, as my intent was not to embarrass the individuals placed on probation. I have also altered or changed the names of some of my colleagues/probation officers, as they wish to remain anonymous.

Valerie, Nuts, and Diane, you fill my emotional bucket and have since the very first time we met over 35 years ago. You continue to be a source of kindness, love, and mostly share in my ability to laugh and keep my sense of humor. We have been through a great deal together, not just through our journey as probation officers, but sharing in life's ups and downs; births of our children, nieces and nephews, cancer, surgeries, finding love, enduring the loss of love, loss of family members, and the loss of some of our *sisters in arms*. I lovingly refer to these women as the *"BITCHES OF BEXAR COUNTY,"* hence the title of the book.

Special thanks and appreciation are extended to the "bitchettes," S.K., L. Rod., Missy B., Jenny G., Norm, A.C., and Corny. You joined our nest without judgment and have added so much joy to my life. I look forward to sharing the next 50 years laughing with y'all while continuing to make memories together.

Heavenly hugs to Geller and Mc Cracken. You are missed beyond measure, and your memories that we share will live in our hearts forever.

Friendship is a part of life; this fact is true, nothing unusual about friends or friendships. The bitches of Bexar County are no different from any other group of friends. It is, however, an interesting one. The profession we chose was one of service, but it came with an emotional and sometimes dangerous faction. We had each other's backs, and for that, I am forever grateful. Looking back on it all, I know now that I could *not* have done life without each and every one of you.

A *huge* shout out to mi familia! My brother-in-law, Tim, to my sister, Leigh, along with my niece and nephew, Andrew and Sarah, thanks for listening, sharing your ideas, and offering your support while writing this book. Thanks to Jeff, Sushi roll, and Emily for helping with the edits, but mostly for being my cheerleaders, not letting me give up on this dream of mine. This has been a labor of love for over 10 years, and you encouraged me every step of the way. Finally, to Todd, my brother from another mother: Thanks for helping me see this book through a reader's eye. Your notes were very much appreciated. You are the Thelma to my Louise, the yin to my yang, and the gin to my tonic. My life would not have been nearly as much fun without you sharing in the laughter and a few tears. It's been a *great* ride.

Trigger Warnings & Disclaimers: *This book contains emotionally heavy or graphic material, including violence and abuse, which may be distressing for some readers.*

PREFACE

Crime is a fascinating topic; it always has been and most likely will continue to be. From the first crime novels like "The Rector of Veilbye," by Steen Steensen Blicher, or Edgar Allan Poe's short story, "The Murders in the Rue Morgue," 1841. The first American crime-related show aired on NBC in 1948: Barney Blake's "Police Reporter." Years later, the ever-popular first true one-hour-long legal drama, still in syndication today, "Perry Mason," debuted in 1957.

I can't begin to list the many crime-related and true crime shows that are currently streaming, as there are literally hundreds. All the major networks during prime time have crime-related television shows, while bookstores have their own sections devoted to the genre. Countless movies revolve around crime, some factual, some fictional, but they are usually a huge draw at the box office. The daily news is riddled with tales of crimes being committed even as I write this. The most popular podcasts are those that have a crime theme as well.

We all know about the ever-present roles of prosecution and defense attorneys in the field of crime, along with the police department, including detectives and the forensic team, and the medical examiner's ability to help solve a crime with the tiniest amount of evidence. There is, however, very little ever said about the work that probation officers perform. What exactly does a probation officer do?

Criminals come in all shapes and sizes, metaphorically, of course. Here are some stories that involve a forgotten aspect of dealing with everyday crime and criminals, and the unsung heroes/heroines who help to rehabilitate members of society. These, my dear readers, are *officers of the court, protectors of society, a.k.a. probation officers.*

A BLONDE WITH A BADGE

First day jitters. I had just relocated from the Dallas Metroplex to San Antonio, Texas. Not knowing what to do with my nervous energy, I couldn't sit still. I hoisted myself up out of the wobbly chair positioned in a narrow hallway and began to pace. Wearing a new Brooks Brothers navy suit, pantyhose, and high heels, I felt out of my league. I was accustomed to my jeans and tennis shoes, but here I was, feeling more and more uncomfortable with each passing moment. I tried to pass the time by approaching a bulletin board that hung on the wall opposite the chair. A newspaper clipping with bold print dangled sadly and without purpose in the center of the board. I leaned in closer to make sure my eyes were not deceiving me. The bold print read:

"DECAPITATED! HEAD FOUND"

OK ..., you now have my FULL attention.

My curiosity piqued as I continued to read. The Dallas Morning News reports a woman walking her dog…

Isn't it always someone walking their dog?

"An unidentified woman discovers a severed head in a remote area of Dallas. The body of the victim is not in the same area. However, reports of the victim's body were later discovered in a different location in the Dallas metroplex. Authorities are not releasing the name of the victim, pending notification of the next of kin. The victim's body had a badge in the right pocket, an adult probation officer's badge. The officer had been performing home visits of his defendants assigned to his caseload in the southern part of Dallas. Co-workers reported the officer had not returned to work; the officer had been missing for a few days before his head and body were located."

What in the ever-loving…

I felt as if I had been engulfed in a time warp. My hands grew clammy, my neck began to sweat, and I could feel my throat closing. All the moisture in my mouth had dissipated, and I felt nauseous. This was to be my *first* day as an adult probation officer! What in God's name had I gotten myself into?

Suddenly, a large man bumped into me, neglecting to say, excuse me, sorry, or even acknowledge my existence at all. I jolted back into reality as the typical office background buzz filled my senses: people conversing back and forth, legal terms being thrown about with ease (words I have only heard on TV), the clicking of computer keyboards, busy footsteps on the linoleum floor, the smell of freshly brewed coffee, and the irritating humming of the fluorescent lights.

A burst of laughter coming from the office nearest to where I was standing rang in my ear. The door of the office suddenly swung open with such velocity that the door handle banged the adjacent wall, swinging back, and hitting the man's shoulder standing in the doorway. Three men follow the first, laughing loudly as they pass by me, one at a time, with no acknowledgement.

Their obnoxious laughter echoed down the hallway as they made lunchtime plans. They went about their daily business, whatever that entailed. I looked back at the open office door and noticed a man seated behind a desk, the man who had hired me. He motioned me in and offered a cup of coffee, which I eagerly accepted. He welcomed me into the department, and I was escorted to an upstairs room where I had my photo taken.

They presented me with my ID, so it must be official.

I was now one of 3,500 adult probation officers in the great state of Texas. Next stop, the *Big Boss's* office. I am ushered in to meet the chief of probation. His secretary, Ava, showed me to a seat and said the Chief would be with me soon. I heard laughter coming from his office, and I heard a woman's giggle in tandem with a man's voice. Finally, the office door opened, and a woman emerged. She was tall, brunette, and was also wearing a suit and heels. The woman held a compact mirror and was concentrating on fixing her smudged lipstick. The *Big*

Boss, a.k.a. Chief, stood at his door, adjusting the belt of his pants. He then walked over to the waiting area where I sat. I stood and extended my hand as he entered my personal space. The chief bellowed loudly to his secretary, "A blonde! *Finally!* We don't have many blondes in this department… You will be a nice addition to our little family."

Ewwww. Yuck.

The chief ordered me into his inner sanctum and invited me to sit on the couch, as he positioned himself behind a large wooden desk. The couch was so low that I found it difficult to get comfortable. (I was told later that the couch was purposely positioned and slanted so the chief would be able to look up a woman's skirt from his chair behind his desk.) Informalities and niceties were exchanged before Chief leaned over to the intercom and summoned a man named Jimmy. He was one of *many* of Chief's underlings and was one of the supervisors assigned to the Misdemeanor division (FYI, this department had supervisors for supervisors). Jimmy ran into the office as if the Pope himself were waiting for him.

"Yeah, Chief? What can I do for you?" Jimmy eagerly asked.

The chief pointed to me with a Cheshire cat grin on his face. "Jimmy, this one's for you…" Jimmy smiled and nervously shook my hand, inviting me to follow him. I awkwardly pulled myself off the couch to the best of my ability and followed Jimmy. As it turns out, this man would be in my life for many years to come…not good, not bad, just ever-present. I was almost out the door when I heard Chief exclaim, "Oh, wait!"

I turned around as the chief tossed me something he retrieved from his desk drawer. He winked and said, "Welcome to Bexar (pronounced Bear) County." The heavy item landed in my hand, and I turned it over to reveal a badge, an adult probation officer badge.

WELCOME TO HELL

Jimmy was a tall, slender man who giggled nervously a lot for no reason. He was awkward, but very kind. Jimmy resided with his mother, never dated, never married, and had no children. He didn't drink or cuss and was a gentleman through and through. He loved the outdoors and often visited his brother's family in Wyoming.

I had to walk fast since it seemed Jimmy was in a hurry to show me the secretarial pool. The secretarial pool was a beehive of working women, centered in the middle of the second floor. The vast room was littered with desks, file cabinets, computers, printers, and typewriters. Jimmy introduced me to the head of the secretaries, Stella, who eyed me up and down while barking out orders to a shy, unassuming woman in the typing pit. She pointed to a wall full of filing cabinets to show me where the supplies were.

Which file cabinet I would need to retrieve supplies from was still unclear.

Jimmy was off again, with me in tow, trying to keep up with his pace. As we passed the elevator, two women emerged; they were from the secretarial pool. I smiled and said, "Good morning!" The women snickered under their breath, but I still heard, "Oh look, a new one…" Apparently, there was a mentality among the officers and the secretaries of *us vs. them*. Walking through a labyrinth of halls, officers were busy in their offices, phones ringing, interviewing defendants, and laughter flowing into the halls as they visited amongst one another.

I use the term 'offices' loosely. The office walls did not reach the ceiling. You could hear everything that was being said. There was no privacy at all. I was told it was for security purposes, and no doors were permitted. Each 'office' space consisted of a desk, an officer's chair, a file cabinet, two chairs for defendants, and a trash can. My bathroom at home was larger than the office I was assigned to.

The actual office building had historical relevance. At one time, it was said to have been a brothel, whore house, house of ill repute… You get the idea. Fitting huh? I was told the San Antonio Fire Department had condemned the structure; annual inspections failed year after year. The building had numerous plumbing issues, was deemed a fire hazard, and yet there were still hundreds of people in and out of it on Dolorosa St., 52 weeks a year, rain or shine.

The building was downtown, a few blocks from the courthouse and near the infamous Riverwalk, so escape to some beautiful areas was easily available. Numerous mom-and-pop Tex-Mex eateries were at our disposal for the ever-popular breakfast tacos or the greasy, cheesy lunch enchiladas. At the end of this maze, Jimmy ushered me into an empty office at the start of another endless hallway. He instructed me to make myself comfortable, and Betty B., my immediate supervisor, would be in to introduce herself and show me the ropes of Misdemeanor County Court at Law No. 9 (CC #9).

I would find out quickly that CC #9 was the court that no one wished upon their worst enemy; it was translated to the *COURT FROM HELL*, and it held up to that reputation. Not because of the officers or the supervisors, but because of the caseload, which was double, if not triple, that of the other courts. Nine county courts handled misdemeanor cases, and ten district courts handled felony cases. The typical number of officers assigned to each court was eight. Our court, however, had fifteen.

County Court at Law No. 9 also handled *all* the misdemeanor domestic violence cases, which would prove to be a challenge, mainly due to the climate of the time. The domestic violence cases were becoming the crime du jour, due to a little ole former football player, Heisman trophy recipient. You might remember *the* O.J. Simpson? That case brought awareness across the country of the importance of the due diligence of crime scene investigations, testimony, and indictment of domestic violent crimes.

As a misdemeanor officer, my caseload included crimes of family/ domestic assaults, DWIs, prostitution, possession of small amounts of marijuana, burglary of a vehicle, failure to ID, public lewdness, unlawful carrying a weapon, and my personal favorite, abuse of a corpse. Yep, that is correct. At this time in Texas, abuse of a corpse was *just* a misdemeanor. (In 2017, the Texas Legislature changed the punishment, increasing the charge from a misdemeanor to a state jail felony.)

I assume that since the victims can't complain, well, then…

County Court at Law No. 9 officers may have had triple the workload, but they were never offered extra compensation. The judges elected to this court were also an interesting group of humanoids and had little respect for us probation officers. They regularly ignored our presence, along with the attorneys, while we were in the courtroom. We were also recipients of the rickety old furniture from other county buildings when those buildings were furnished with all-new furniture. I respectfully referred to us as the *Red Headed Stepchildren of Probation* because we were treated as such. (No offense to my auburn allies… There are few, but they are mighty.)

What did I do to deserve this?

Work conditions were poor, and the pay was awful. Respect and morals were low. So, why do this job?

During the early 1990s, Texas employed approximately 3,500 adult probation officers, so we were a tight-knit sisterhood/brotherhood. Adult probation officers were required to have completed a four-year undergraduate college degree in either social work, criminal justice, political science, or psychology. Many officers had master's degrees, and a few had Ph.D.s. These officers were employed throughout the 254 counties of the great state of Texas. These numbers did not include the juvenile or federal systems. The average length of employment as a probation officer is three years. Burnout occurs quickly as the job is highly demanding. The caseloads were brutal, work conditions were unfavorable, and the pay was a joke. Not to mention simultaneously dealing with the judges' and attorneys' egos, and the chief and his little minions' *bigger* egos. Adult probation officer pay in the early 90s was $24,000. Many officers had second jobs just to cover living expenses. Sadly, even today (2026), pay for state and county probation officers remains very low, while pay for federal probation officers is, of course, more than exemplary.

A woman quickly shuffled into the office where I was waiting. She placed a large stack of files on her desk and said, "I'm Betty! Welcome!"

Betty B., County Court at Law No. 9 supervisor, was a pleasant, exuberant individual with a small frame, a great laugh, and a fabulous sense of humor. I soon found out that if you didn't possess that sense of humor, you would *not* survive this job. Betty B. had the energy of 50 people and could handle anything. She could multi-task her way out of a monsoon and make it look easy. Betty walked over to the chair I was sitting in and tapped my hand gingerly.

"Let me introduce you around," she told me.

As we turned to exit her office, an attractive woman was yelling at the top of her lungs at the end of the long hallway.

"FUCK YOU, BETTY! I'M NOT GOING! YOU CAN SEND THE BOYS."

Betty looked at me without skipping a beat, smiled, and said, "Someone doesn't want to go back to the courthouse."

Betty introduced me to Libby, one of fourteen new colleagues that I would be working with. Upon meeting Libby, she mumbled, "Oh great, another blue-eyed blonde..."

What? The Chief said there weren't that many blondes!

"My eyes are green, NOT blue!" I blurted out.

Where did that come from?

Without thinking, the snarky retort escaped my lips. I was rude to another human on my first day at the department. In an instant, I learned to stick up for myself.

Betty smiled at me and said, "You are going to work out just fine, you're a great fit for this court."

I was introduced to the rest of the crew and escorted to the end of the hall, where my office was located. I had the misfortune of being housed next to Tayla, the woman who was recently yelling at my new supervisor. Tayla would be my neighbor.

UH OH!

She was a feisty gal. She loved to drink her lunch and carried on her drinking shenanigans at downtown bars after work. On numerous days, Tayla would be wearing the same suit she had worn the previous day. (Not judging, just saying.) She avoided me like the plague for the first few months, never warming up to me. Tayla soon went on to 'greener' pastures, becoming a federal probation officer. (God help us all, and God bless Texas).

Years later, I learned that she had consumed too much alcohol and driven her and her husband off an overpass, landing safely below. Tayla recovered, went on to work for a few more years before suffering from a fatal heart attack, and died in her mid-40s

Another interesting colleague I was introduced to on my first day was Tiffany. Her office was located two doors down from mine. You couldn't help but notice a rather large bouquet of flowers and three 8 x 10 framed, professional-colored photographs of three very handsome, but different men positioned on Tiffany's credenza. It turned out that Tiffany was promised to be engaged to *two* of these photographed men and was dating the third. Tiffany's office was located near the end of the hall. If one of her suitors came calling, we were instructed to run and tell her which man was there, so the superlative photos could be removed and her appropriate jewelry, given by the appointed suitors, could be switched out. Tiffany was a thin, pretty girl with porcelain, flawless skin. Although I didn't agree with her dating philosophy, we grew to become frenemies, and I did enjoy her company, in moderation.

On one occasion, though, I made the mistake of telling Tiffany about my crush on a certain prosecutor assigned to our court. The very next day, after I had expressed my affection for this person, Tiffany pranced into my office, telling me about her activities of the prior evening. Gleefully, she bragged about her, and this certain prosecutor attending a Spurs basketball game, followed by a romantic dinner in front of a roaring fire, and, well, you use your imagination for the rest.

Promised to be engaged to two men, dating a *third*, and now she's homing in on *my* crush. Let it be known, I would never be that naive and divulge my feelings about anyone else to her ever, ever again. Tiffany eventually married one of the fab three, divorced him, quit her job as a probation officer, and has since remarried and resides somewhere in Texas.

Huey, Duey, and Luey, the three amigos, were also assigned to County Court at Law No. 9. Their offices were located across the hall from mine. Over time, I noticed that they didn't have much of a caseload and weren't assigned courthouse duties, but they did report to work each day. Their day consisted of playing cards, wandering next door to Panchito's for a two-hour breakfast, returning to play more cards, disappearing for a two-hour lunch, returning and continuing the card game until 4:30, then calling it a day and going home.

On my first encounter with one of these men, I simply asked, "So… what is it that you do here?" Huey smirked and replied, "Don't worry about it, little lady. It is none of your concern."

He winked at me as he walked away.

Curious about these guys, I asked other officers who had been in the court for some time for the scoop.

"Oh, them? They know the chief."

I shrugged my shoulders in confusion and asked for more information.

"The less you know, the better."

As it turned out, the three amigos were the hunting faction of the department. Each one owned land for hunting. Deer, hogs, turkey, birds, you name it, Chief shot it. The chief loved hunting, and these three accommodated that urge for him and his underlings during hunting seasons. In return, they weren't obligated to do any work and were paid a handsome salary for hunting services rendered.

Other than Huey, Duey, and Luey, each officer was assigned a *Duty Day* once a month. After I had some training under my belt, it was my turn to be added to the rotation. The duties involved answering the phone, making appointments for officers, and performing other mundane tasks while the other probation officers (POs) were out to lunch for that day. On one particular *Duty Day* months later, while answering the phone, our judge summoned the three amigos to the courthouse immediately.

"Yes!" I thought to myself. Finally, they will have to do some work. Au contraire. The three amigos returned three hours later, boasting that Judge had taken them to lunch at the Petroleum Club, of which Judge was an elite member. Not only did these boys *not* have to work because they were buddies with Chief, but they were also having martini lunches with the judge. I really resented these three. They were lazy, entitled, and possessed a machismo philosophy of women that consisted of the following: Women are put on this earth to cook, clean the household, provide salacious services to the male species, raise their offspring, and not ask any questions.

I was raised in West Texas, where women ruled the roost. We were revered, treated with respect, and had doors opened for us. I had a difficult time wrapping my brain around this methodology. I had to see these three idiots every single workday, but eventually I learned the best thing to do was ignore them. Years later, the three amigos were split up and reassigned to other courts, and out of CC #9. I have to say, I did not miss them.

So, to answer the earlier question about why on God's green Earth I worked as a probation officer… The answer is relatively easy. I had the time of my life!

I could not wait to get to work. I never knew what was going to come across my desk or who I would meet next. My morbid fascination got the best of me, and I was curious about the crimes the defendants committed. The biggest plus of working as a probation officer was my colleagues. They are some of the coolest people on this planet, many of whom I remain close to. Some of us have known each other for 35 years and are still holding strong.

I have no idea why I was placed in CC #9, but this would be my work home for many years to come until my so-called promotion (I use this term loosely) to the felony courts. I gained many positive insights from my time assigned to this court. I learned to cuss like a sailor, how to stand up for myself, and I also found my voice. But most importantly, I found the women in my life with whom I now share an eternal and perpetual bond after many decades of friendship.

SO...YOU WANT TO
BE ON PROBATION?

The day arrives when the defendant has appeared in court for the crime they committed, and now "punishment" or "consequences" await them. Should an individual commit a misdemeanor, the consequences are as follows: the defendant will either serve 1 year in the county jail or be granted probation. If probation is granted, the defendant will be required to serve 2 years of misdemeanor probation. If a felony has been committed, the consequences are 5 to 95 years in state prison, or, if placed on probation, the defendant will have to serve up to 10 years on felony probation.

Misdemeanor or felony offenders who are placed on probation are then read *the rules,* a.k.a., conditions of probation. These *rules* simply translate into the court-mandated guidelines that each defendant on probation must follow. If a defendant has a minor misdemeanor, such as driving while their license is suspended, all the way to the worst possible crime committed, such as felonies, murder, child abuse, drug trafficking, human trafficking, etc., there is absolutely no allowance for any deviation from the rules. Below, the legal jargon has been omitted to make it easier for the layperson to understand.

The general rules must all be followed by each defendant, and they are as follows:

1. Don't get any new arrest/if you are arrested for any new crime, advise your probation officer (PO) immediately. Don't lie to your PO. We don't like it, and we will find out if you are lying to us about any and all of your prior arrests or any new ones. Arrests must be reported to the PO immediately.

2. Abstain from the illegal use of controlled substances and dangerous drugs, nor use of alcoholic beverages; defendants will submit to drug tests, and urine samples will be collected from the defendant to test for illegal substances. (Fyi, the defendant pays for the drug tests.)

3. Avoid hanging out with folks who have criminal records and who you know may sell illegal substances; they can get you into trouble. Don't go to places where you know that controlled substances and dangerous drugs are illegally possessed, sold, or used.

4. Keep gainful employment in a lawful occupation. You must show proof of employment. If you are unemployed, we will refer you to a job counselor to help you find employment.

5. Defendants must report in person as directed by their probation officer. This may be daily, weekly, or monthly, and you should conduct yourself in a proper and orderly manner while reporting.

6. Permit the probation/supervision officer or their assistants to transport you as needed and visit you in your home or elsewhere (by the way, we don't have to inform you when we are coming, and we don't need a search warrant either, so just be ready.) We may search your person, vehicle, place of residence, and any contraband found in your possession will be subject to confiscation. Contraband includes prohibited or illegal weapons, controlled substances or illegal drugs, pornographic materials, and obscene devices.

7. Remain in Bexar County unless you have written consent from your probation officer or the judge.

8. Do not leave the great state of Texas without the written consent of the court.

9. Support your dependents that you now have or that you may acquire during your term on probation.

10. Provide any proof of residence. If you move, notify the probation officer immediately of any change to your address/phone number. New employment or any new arrest must be reported to your probation officer within 48 hours.

The conditions of probation consisted of seven pages, and each defendant must be read the rules so they may fully understand their responsibilities before signing on the dotted line and taking responsibility for following them. The defendant is advised that if these rules are *not* followed, the court will issue the appropriate punishment. The punishment range is huge, from a simple admonishment from the judge (a.k.a., a slap on the wrist) to possible jail time to get the defendant's attention, and an additional class might benefit the defendant.

Since new defendants were placed on probation daily, *the rules* had to be read to newly granted defendants each day. This meant that probation officers assigned to each court would meet in the second-floor conference room to read these rules to new defendants embarking on their probation journey.

The large conference room had a slope in the floor. I was always nervous that the floor would collapse, with the weight of all the people in the room, and we would end up on the first floor. The linoleum had been repaired numerous times by adding more tiles on top of the broken tiles, resulting in broken shoe heels and sprained ankles. Not only was the conference room used to read the newbie defendants the conditions of probation, but it was also where I met my colleagues, my bitches in arms. Many became fast and loyal friends.

MISDEMEANOR MEMORIES, NO APPOINTMENT NECESSARY

As I mentioned, my caseload was large. The largest I recall was 400 human beings, whom I was legally responsible for. Officers' caseloads in other courts consisted of only 150 individuals. Quite a discrepancy, I would say (you need to know that the great state of Texas has since stepped in and now allows an officer to oversee approximately 150 defendants at a time).

My duties as a misdemeanor officer included overseeing 400-plus defendants, each of whom had to be seen in person at least once a month. I was to administer drug tests to these individuals and ensure they didn't violate any more laws. I also had to make sure they were employed in a *legal* occupation, were paying or current on their child support, and, if deemed necessary, that fines, court costs, fees, etc., were paid and up to date. Most importantly, I had to make sure the defendants were attending court-mandated courses/classes, such as rehab (AA, NA), or performing community service. I was also expected to be in court for courthouse duties for one week each month, every other month. This job taught me how to multitask my ass off, which I am grateful for, because I can now juggle numerous things thanks to the skills I gained at County Court at Law No. 9.

Probation departments throughout Texas had already adopted the appointment system in the late 80s and early 90s. Defendants would set up scheduled times to visit their assigned officers, making everyone's life just a little easier. But *not* Bexar County, oh no, they hadn't stepped into the twentieth century by utilizing the appointment system. This simply meant that the defendants in Bexar County could show up at the office whenever they wanted. This resulted in a very frustrating, unorganized use of our time.

Operating hours for the department were Monday through Friday, 7:00 a.m. to 6:00 p.m. Mayhem and chaos would ensue as defendants who had put off visiting their assigned officers would magically appear at 5:00 p.m. on the last weekday of the month, waiting to see their officers, and guess what? The Bexar County Adult Probation Department office closed at 6:00 p.m. The line of defendants resembled a crowd at a PINK concert, with people wrapping around the building. County Court at Law Number 9 always had the highest number of people needing to be seen before the end of the month.

Calculate, if you will, fifteen officers, minus Huey, Duey, and Luey. Each had approximately 400 people on their caseloads. On the last day of the month and in the last hour, security monitors would blast over the PA, "ALL AVAILABLE OFFICERS REPORT TO CC#9 TO HELP WITH REPORTS." Ridiculous, stupid, idiotic, abomination, and yet, the process continued month after month, year after year, until one day an idea was born.

Valerie, one of the bitches, who had recently transferred from a neighboring probation department in the next county, shared that those appointments had been a part of their everyday practices. Valerie suggested to the administration that using the appointment system would benefit both the officer and the defendant, saving everyone time and money. Admin listened, then placed it in the *"don't give a shit, and we're not going to even think about doing this"* file.

Months passed, and a department meeting was called; mandatory attendance by all officers was expected. During this meeting, the chief opened the floor for comments, concerns, or ideas for the probation department. Henry, a male officer, stood up and suggested we might want to implement an appointment system, which had proved productive in other counties across Texas. Well, lo and behold—the male figure spoke, so it shall come to pass! The appointment system was adopted and put into our daily practice the following week.

Penises - 1, vaginas - 0

I quickly learned that the male species always overrode the female species in the department. At this point in my life, I had not found my 'voice' and was still too timid to speak up for myself or for the women in the department. I eventually got to a point where I wasn't going to take @#$%*^ anymore. I did speak up, and I can say the administration did not like me because of it.

Miss Congeniality was never going to be on my resume with the department.

MACHO, MACHO MAN!

The machismo, egocentric world in which I had been indoctrinated and employed in the early 90s was a male-dominated workplace. I quickly realized that women had no voice. We were to do as we were told: don't ask questions, wear pantyhose and high heels, look pretty, and smile.

I was made aware, after months of employment, that Chief offered certain women *promotions* and *financial rewards*, a.k.a. raises, if *certain favors* were bestowed upon him. Men in the department would be rewarded if they took Chief hunting or gifted him with guns. The chief loved guns, and I found this to be true in my first week at the department. This is how I learned this fun little fact: While seated at my desk, trying to figure out the court schedule, I was approached by three men in suits. The men didn't introduce themselves as one man stepped forward.

He did not smile and, in a low, deep voice, said, "I understand you didn't contribute the $75 donation for Chief's birthday."

Short and handsome pulled a photo of a gun from his suit pocket, showing me what I assumed to be the gun we officers were to purchase for the chief.

I replied, "This is my first week, and I've not received my first paycheck."

Short and handsome stated, "When you receive your first paycheck, please bring $75 to Ava, the chief's secretary."

The three men turned in unison and retreated from my office.

"SEVENTY-FIVE DOLLARS???? Are you kidding me?" I almost blurted out.

Did they know the starting salary for a new hire? I immediately found Betty B., my supervisor, to question if this was the norm. Betty advised me that, yes, officers were expected to contribute towards Chief's birthday presents.

She then laughed and said, "Just wait and see what he wants us to buy him for Christmas."

Not thirty minutes later, my office desk phone rang. Chief's voice was on the other end.

"Little lady, could you come up to my office for a quick chat?"

"Sure, Sir, I'm on my way," I replied.

Taking the flight of stairs, I sprinted up to my new boss's office. Ava was waiting for me. She opened the door of Chief's office to reveal the *goon squad*. Two of whom were seated on the couch, and *short and handsome* stood by Chief, like a Bailiff in a courtroom. Ava glanced my way with a scared look on her face. Our eyes locked as she closed the door. My inner voice was yelling, "HELP ME!!!! ANYBODY!!"

Not invited to sit, the Chief said, "I know this is your first week, and ya haven't got'n your first pay. No worries, but I hired you, and twice a year these gentlemen are kind enough to pay me back for hiring you all by collecting some fun mun so I can buy me a little sometin, sometin, for myself. Seventy-five dollars to Ava once you are paid, OK?"

As there was no moisture in my mouth, my reply was a soft whisper. "Got it, Chief."

Goon number one stood to let me out of the inner sanctum. I felt as if I were in a *Twilight Zone* episode as I walked into Ava's office. She didn't say anything and couldn't even look at me. I could not get back to my office fast enough.

I called my sister, Leigh, in North Carolina, to convey the recent events. She was speechless.

"What in the world, Pam? They really expect that kind of money to be spent on the head cheese? Seventy-five dollars is a lot of money.

I could understand $10, but whoa!!"

She was more concerned that the chief called me into his office on my first week.

"Are you ok?" Leigh asked.

"Yeah, I will be fine," I told her.

"I worry about you. Wish I were there to give you a hug."

"Me too, Sis, me too."

ADULT VS. JUVENILE

In Texas, in the realm of the criminal justice world, a 17-year-old is considered an adult, whereas a person who is 16 and younger is termed a juvenile.

A 17-year-old who is considered an adult and commits a crime will face harsher laws and punishments; these laws are designed to protect society. Juveniles, the youth, 16 and younger, have less harsh laws/punishments that are designed to protect the child, not society.

Example: if an adult defendant commits a misdemeanor, the punishment is up to 2 years on probation or up to 1 year in the county jail.

For felony cases, which are more serious offenses, the punishment for a 17-year-old adult ranges from probation for up to 10 years to up to 99 years in the state prison system.

HOW YOU GET DEAD IN TEXAS

I have experienced some strange things in my life, but one of the strangest was while in a district/felony court, where I was able to hear a death sentence being handed down to a defendant. I know that all of us will face the day when we are no longer on this earth, the day we die. For the most part, we do not know the day or time of this event, but if you are a person who has committed capital murder, you will be privy to this information.

How odd, right? To hear the day and time of your demise.

The jury reached a unanimous verdict, and the accused was found guilty. This same jury also had the power to decide whether the defendant would be executed or not. The sentence hearing was held on another day, and this being the last day of the capital case, so as you can imagine, the courtroom was sure to be packed. Families, friends, curious onlookers, and the news media, touting their cameras and microphones, were all present to witness the sentencing.

On this day, extra bailiffs are called in for added security, standing at attention, watching the anxious crowd awaiting the judge's arrival. Judge enters, we all stand, he/she motions for all to be seated, he/she then will give the reason why all have gathered, and he/she asks the victim's families and friends to step to the podium. They will be allowed to address the defendant; this is called the Victim Impact Statement. Stories are told of the loved ones who became victims of the horrible crimes and how the family had to endure the pain and suffering, all because of the defendant's actions. Photos are sometimes shared of the deceased victim, as many tears are shed; it is truly one of the saddest things I have ever witnessed. Sometimes the defendant will cry, and sometimes they appear angry. The worst reaction is when they do not react, but instead just sit there, flanked by three bailiffs, not able to look those poor people in the eye.

Does the defendant even care, or are they so scared that they simply can't react because they are in disbelief that they themselves are responsible for this circus?

Then the judge asks the defendant to stand with his/her defense attorney and the prosecutor. Judges will sometimes lecture on the atrocities and the impact the crime has had on the community. I witnessed a judge forcing the defendant to face his/her own mother and father, saying, "See what you have done? Look at the lives you've destroyed?"

The judge will then say to the accused something like: "John Doe, you have been charged with, blah, blah, the crime of capital murder, your punishment will be carried out on such date at 6:00 p.m. You will be executed by lethal injection until you are dead. May God have mercy on your soul. Bailiff, please escort John Doe out."

The defendant is then whisked off to the holding cell while the sounds of muffled sniffles and crying are heard echoing in the courtroom. Bailiff announces, "All rise," and Judge exits. Hugs are exchanged among family and friends as the extra bailiffs remain in the courtroom to ensure fights do not break out. The news media gather up their equipment, boxing up cameras and electric cords. The crowd then flows out in a quiet trance, whispering ever so softly. Some are in tears, while others are high-fiving each other.

Eventually, the courtroom is emptied, and I feel a cold, hollow feeling. What did I just experience, I wonder. It is indescribable sitting in the back row on the hard wooden pew of the courtroom, absorbing all that had just transpired.

I remember walking back to the office, listening to the birds chirp, feeling the warmth of the sun on my skin, appreciating the bustle of cars on the streets, and watching people go about their day, unaware of what I had just experienced. Life does truly go on.

The death penalty has been around since the beginning of time; whatever your opinion on this topic, it is sure to be a personal one. The debate for or against taking someone's life, whether it be sanctioned by the state or by the federal government, will always be a hot topic. Let's be real here, the death penalty is purely good old-fashioned revenge.

Texas has the dubious and illustrious honor of being called the *execution capital of the world.* The number of executions has decreased in our state, but capital murders are still being committed. The average cost to execute a defendant is approximately $2 million dollars... per person... crazy, huh? This economic fact is the same for all the states; this is a solid reason why many states have opted out of the execution process, as it is just too costly to execute people. Taxpayers' dollars could be spent on other things.

Before Texas became a state in 1845, we were the Republic of Texas. Yep, we were our own little country. Fun fact: the Texas flag is allowed to fly at the same height/mast as the American flag because of this.

Before and after becoming a state, Texas's method of execution was exclusively hanging; we did, however, use the firing squad for a man who committed the crime of rape, as well as during the Civil War for three Confederate deserters.

The first man to die by hanging in Texas was in Bolivar Pass in 1819. George Brown was hanged for the crime of piracy, stealing from a ship at sea.

The first woman hanged lived near the Aransas River, Texas. Chipita Rodriguez was described as a small, frail, and older woman who lived alone in a log cabin. Traveling lodgers would stay in her home for a hot meal and a place to sleep before continuing their journey. On one such occasion, a man carrying $600 worth of gold in his knapsack spent an evening with Chipita. She discovered the gold and decided to take it for herself. She fed the man a hot meal, prepared his bed, and waited for the lodger to fall asleep. While in a deep slumber, Chipita killed the man with an axe, then stuffed his body in a burlap sack, throwing the man's remains into the nearby Aransas River. The remains of the recent deceased were discovered a few days later, floating down the river. It was traced back to Chipita, and she was ultimately convicted and hanged in 1863.

At one point in the history of the United States, every state utilized one of five methods of execution: firing squad, lethal gas, hanging, electric chair, and lethal injection. The Furman v. Georgia case raised questions about the death penalty. In 1972, the United States Supreme Court suspended executions, ruling that the death penalty laws were unconstitutional as well as cruel and unusual punishment, halting all forms of execution.

In the 1970s, Gary Gilmore from Utah had been convicted of killing two men and was found guilty of capital murder, ultimately being sentenced to death. Due to the 1972 moratorium, Mr. Gilmore's death sentence would not come to fruition, but Gary wanted to die. He had two failed suicide attempts while in prison before he pleaded his case in November 1976 to the board of pardons. Eventually, Gary's wish was granted, and his execution would be carried out on a cold, blistery morn on January 17, 1977, by a group of volunteer police officers via a firing squad. His last words were, "Let's do it."

The execution was an event heard around the world; executions then resumed in the United States to the disappointment of every person on death row, thinking they had been rescued from this fate.

[Sidebar: Dan Wiedner, founder of Wiedner + Kennedy, found inspiration from Gilmore's last words and adapted them for the 1988 Nike campaign slogan, "Just Do it." Creepy but creative in its own right.]

At the time of this publication, twenty-seven states are currently using executions in the United States. Lethal injection is the method of choice; however, should this procedure be found to be unconstitutional for whatever reason, a backup method will be made available.

Texas's death penalty has an interesting history. We have utilized three methods, and they are in order as follows:

*HANGING-1819-1923 (1,343 men executed by this method and one woman).

*ELECTRIC CHAIR-1924-1964 (361 men executed by this method, no women).

*LETHAL INJECTION-Adopted in 1977, however, not used until 1982, still the preferred method of execution today. (As of April 2025, 584 men and nine women have been executed via lethal injection.)

Texas's first method of execution was that of hanging. The hangings were to be carried out on Saturdays at high noon at the county courthouse or town square, and each county was responsible for its own executions. The public was allowed to bear witness along with the judge and the county sheriff. Families would come by horse and buggy from nearby farms to purchase monthly supplies, visit with family and friends, witness the execution, and attend church the following day. These events were carnival-like, with vendors selling their tonics and wares, and sweet treats for the children.

The accused's hands were bound and tied behind their back, and they would be placed on the back of a horse while the hangman's noose was placed around the defendant's neck. Each knot represented a certain amount of weight, so the more knots there were, the heavier the person was. The defendant might have a bag placed over their face to hide the horrors that will be on the suspect's face. The judge would read aloud to the anxious crowd the crime committed by the accused, as adults listened while children laughed and played with their friends, unaware of what was about to happen to the man on the horse. The county sheriff would then slap the backside of the horse, encouraging the horse to run, leaving the defendant to dangle until he/she died.

Should a tree be unavailable, which isn't unusual in the panhandle of Texas, the method of hanging used was to stand the accused on top of an overturned tin bucket, the defendant's hands bound, while trying to balance their feet on the bucket. At the same time, the rope was placed around the neck, and the other end of the rope was tossed over a large wooden makeshift hangman's apparatus. At the appointed time, the sheriff would kick the bucket out from under the defendant as spectators patiently watched and waited for death to appear and stop the wriggling of the person at the end of the noose. Death would not come quickly, as this form of lynching could take up to ten minutes as the defendant slowly suffocated.

In modern times, capital crimes in Texas are punishable by either life in prison, without the possibility of parole, or the ultimate punishment, death by lethal injection. Should an individual be seventeen at the time of committing a capital crime, by law, the federal government does not allow the execution of said individual. Instead, they will remain in prison for the remainder of their life without the possibility of parole.

Should an 18-year-old commit a capital offense in Texas, the lethal injection method of execution is, however, a possibility. Texas is, after all, *the execution capital of the world.*

The following are crimes that a capital murderer would commit to be placed on death row in the great state of Texas:

*Killing a judge

*Killing a police officer

*Killing a firefighter

*Killing an EMT (on duty)

*Killing an elderly person (62 years or older)

*Killing a child (10 years or younger)

*Committing two felonies at the same time, with one of those felonies resulting in death.

Example: An individual is killed during the act of being raped, or an individual working as a clerk at a gas station is killed when a suspect shoots and kills the clerk as they are leaving the store with the stolen beer.

I share this bit of historical knowledge about the death penalty with the reader because it is interesting. European countries think of us as barbarians, as they have not used the death penalty for many years. The criminal element walks amongst us every day; these individuals will not be placed on probation. I did meet a few of the men who had committed a capital crime, and I was able to witness a few defendants being interviewed for a pre-sentence investigation report, as Diane, bitch number three, who was a pre-sentence investigation (PSI) officer, invited me along to learn about the process and how she interviewed these capital felons. This pre-sentence report is the biography of the defendant and is used as a source of information for the prison administration when the defendant arrives on death row.

The citizens of Texas take on the responsibility to carry out the death sentence for capital crimes. Texas has a saying, and we Texans live and die by this credo:

"DON'T MESS WITH TEXAS!"

PPG, THE PENILE PLETHYSMOGRAPHY

The penile plethysmography (PPG) is an odd machine; anything with the word 'penile' in it is sure to get anyone's attention. I know it got mine. I hear the PPG isn't utilized in Bexar County anymore, but it was in the early 1990s. Before I became a probation officer, I didn't even know a device like this existed. This machine was used for sex offenders and no one else.

I was invited to witness the machine and its use when I became a felony intensive supervision officer, and I will never forget that afternoon or what transpired from this experience. I felt as if I was walking into a science fiction movie, unable to escape what I was seeing, a nightmare, oddly disturbing and fascinating at the same time. I had been advised that I would be observing a sex offender, a pedophile, a man in his mid-30s who had offended numerous times. His preference was for children, especially young boys and girls.

I entered a room with low ambient lighting, and the air was cold and damp. Men and women were bustling about setting up video equipment and a machine that resembled a polygraph. People were whispering so as not to disturb the room's aura. There was a two-way mirrored window through which we could see into the darkness. I saw a man seated in a metal chair with his back to us, sitting very still, with wires or electrodes attached to his temples, and more wires near his white socked ankles.

I heard a man's voice projecting over an intercom from the room I was standing in. "We are ready to get started. Are you comfortable?"

The man in the chair replied in a low, mellow voice, "Yes."

Without any notice, bright images were projected onto the wall at a slow pace. Images of food, hamburgers, steak, Italian food, cold iced drinks with water droplets forming on the glass, and fresh fruit. I got hungry just watching these photos pass one after the other on the wall. The following projected images were of cars, streets, high-rise buildings, houses, a riding lawn mower, farm equipment, farmland with cotton crops, barns, and farm animals. The last grouping of colorful photos was a child's playground in a neighborhood park with swings and a seesaw in the distance. This rapidly became the elephant in the room. The machines began to make noise, and whispers spread among the facilitators. Photos of a circus, an amusement park, and a carousel followed. The machine was measuring the blood flow to the penis; these images were sexually arousing the man in the chair.

American sex offender treatment programs used the PPG along with district/felony courts as a condition of probation for a sex offender who had received probation or was on the supervised release program. This was used to help monitor a pedophile's sexual behavior to predict possible reoffending deviant sexual behavior by the defendant. The polygraph was also a way to monitor a sex offender. It was by far a less intrusive method to check if there is a threat or a possibility that a sex offender/defendant might reoffend.

I learned a great deal that afternoon. I was reminded of the cruel world that I live in, the atrocities that some innocent children fall prey to, and I just felt heavy and sad.

I never saw the face of the man in the chair that afternoon, which was probably for the best.

MR. MOSES

MR. MOSES — 50
Charged with assault (causing bodily injury)
Class A misdemeanor
No priors. Given 1-year probation

Mr. Moses married his high school sweetheart, and he and Mrs. Moses had recently celebrated 32 years together. Unable to have children of their own, they spent much of their time spoiling their nieces and nephews, taking them on vacations to Disney World and on fishing trips in Colorado. Mr. Moses adored his wife. He spoke of her at every monthly appointment and shared family photos with me. I could feel his admiration for his wife and the life they had built together.

Neither Mr. nor Mrs. Moses could afford college, so they began work straight out of high school. Mr. Moses had worked his way up to the position of a supervisor for a prominent residential builder in San Antonio. Mrs. Moses worked in the corporate offices of H-E-B, a popular grocery chain in the lower regions of Texas. Two people who had worked hard their entire lives, people of faith, respected and loved each other and loved their family. Life circumstances changed in an instant for this couple one Friday night.

Mr. Moses arrived early for his first scheduled meeting. I made a habit of never looking at the police report to see what crime the defendant had committed before meeting them. I introduced myself and motioned for him to take a seat.

"Mr. Moses, you have been placed on probation, and I want to hear the facts of the case from you. In detail, please describe why you are here."

He cleared his throat, looked down at the ground, and proceeded to tell me why.

"Friday is pay day, and the guys and I hang out at Louie's, a bar around the corner from work. The wife wasn't too happy about this, but she always knows where I am, at least on Friday nights."

He was humored by this and chuckled nervously, waiting for me to chuckle with him, but I didn't.

"Continue, Mr. Moses."

"Oh yeah, well you see, this particular night, I stayed later at Louie's than I do normally, Carlos was retiring, and we were just you know, saying our goodbyes." He fidgeted in his chair. "I got home late, really late, and the Mrs. was very upset!!! We're in the kitchen, I'm hungry, scrounging for some tin to eat in the fridge, I close the fridge door, and she stabs me with the scissors."

Mr. Moses pointed to the location on his chest where the scissors entered. I tried not to react, but in my head, I was processing what he was saying and wondering why Mrs. Moses wasn't seated across the desk telling this story. Shouldn't *she* be the one on probation? Not her husband?

"Mr. Moses, what did you do? How did you respond to this?" I asked.

"I grabbed the first thing I could get my hands on, the telephone. I knew this was wrong, but I was in shock, you know? I took the phone and laid one on her, I hit her as hard as I could upside her head."

"Then what happened?" I inquired.

"I dunno, I woke up in the hospital handcuffed to the bed with police officers in my room."

"Is Mrs. Moses ok?"

"Oh yeah," he replied. "She had a big goose egg, though." He chuckled again to himself. "Some doctor person got the scissors out, and he told me how lucky I was, because the scissors almost hit something important."

"Mr. Moses, have you spoken to Mrs. Moses since the incident?"

"Yeah, she picked me up at the hospital, we're fine. I'm back working, but I'm not going to Louie's for a while."

I agreed with Mr. Moses, stating it would be advantageous for him to stay away from any bar or alcohol while he's on probation.

"Remember, Mr. Moses, please no alcohol or illegal drugs while you're on probation."

Mr. Moses completed his year of probation without incident. He completed all his classes, paid his fines, went to AA, and couples therapy with Mrs. Moses.

On his last appointment, Mr. Moses thanked me for helping him traverse a difficult year and said this. "I swung by the hospital and found the doctor who took the scissors out of me. Just wanted to tell him thank you, he saved my life, you know? The wife and I have never been closer, and I owe that to you. You're the one who got us to go to that couples doctor. I didn't believe in that stuff, used to think therapy is for sissies, but you know, I got some tin out of it."

Tears welled in both of our eyes. I asked Mr. Moses if I could hug him, and he obliged me with one of the best bear hugs I have ever received.

DON'T CRY OVER SPILT HOT CHOCOLATE

The CC #9 judge was a control freak. This judge did not allow *anybody* besides them to have beverages in the courtroom. On one occasion, I witnessed Judge hurling a blue enameled water thermos across the bench towards the prosecution table because a prosecutor had a cup of hot tea with lemon to soothe their sore throat.

Judge proclaimed, "I don't care if you have a fever, flu, or pneumonia, get that cup out of my courtroom!"

Not learning from this, I was stupid, and on a blistery winter morning, I brought a steaming cup of hot chocolate into the courtroom. Without paying attention, I placed the cup of hot liquid, with the proper lid attached, next to 50 probation files. My dingbat court partner hurled his briefcase onto the table, knocking over my hot cocoa just as the bailiff announced, "All rise, county court at law number nine is now in session, the honorable *control freak* presides."

Without thinking, I lunged my body with my freshly dry-cleaned, pin-striped, Pima cotton blouse onto the table, soaking up the dark, hot liquid that was ebbing towards the end of the table. Quickly buttoning up my suit jacket to conceal the stain, I approached the bench for the morning's docket.

Yes, I learned my lesson, and I never arrived at court with *any* liquid, foreign, or domestic in my possession. The dry cleaner couldn't remove the stain from my favorite blouse, so I learned two lessons that day.

Control freak - 1, blonde with a badge - 0.

OPEN SESAME

**A warning to the reader: this story is
graphic and may be difficult to read.**

Owen, a man in his early 40s, walked into my office for a misdemeanor charge of driving while his license was suspended. Not an egregious crime by any means, but his story is worth telling. Upon reviewing his case file, I saw that Owen had been a resident for 5 years in one of our many state penitentiaries for a third-degree felony for intoxication assault, ten years before our first encounter. He was paroled early without incident and had not been in the criminal justice system for some time now.

I saw Owen for many months before I found the courage to ask him about his experience in state prison. I was curious because, in my purview as a probation officer, defendants were given a second chance via probation. Their punishment was probation, *not* prison. Should a defendant have a misstep and fall off the probation wagon, then and only then would the defendant go to prison for a felony, so I would see defendants before they went to prison. It wasn't very often that I was able to interview someone under these circumstances.

At one of our appointments, I finally asked Owen questions about his time in Texas prisons. How were his first months? Was the food good or bad? Was the bed comfortable? How did the other inmates treat him? How did he spend his day? Did he work, etc? He was very forthcoming with information, which I was not expecting. Owen stated that, upon reflection, his time in prison wasn't what he had expected. He said he had known of men in his neighborhood who had gone to prison, but did not know firsthand what being locked up behind bars was like until he was sentenced himself.

His mother, on the other hand, had heard horror stories of what takes place in the penitentiaries. She knew her son's journey would not be an easy one, so before her son went to prison, she had Owen go to a family friend and brandish an enormous tattoo of the Virgin Mary on his back. She felt that the figure would watch over and protect her son while he was incarcerated. As he continued the story, he stood tall from his chair in my office, and before I knew what was happening, Owen was taking his shirt off to reveal one of the most beautiful and colorful tattoos that I have ever seen.

He stated his indoctrination into the prison customs and roles of the inmate society happened in his second week in prison. He described the night by saying he found himself in his cell without his cellmate. He said the room felt damp and cold, and something just felt weird. It was almost time for lights out when he suddenly turned to see a group of inmates standing in the doorway.

These men rushed Owen as two of them took charge of each of Owen's arms, while two additional men pushed him onto his knees, shoving his face into the mattress of the lower bunk. He stated his face was being forced so heavily into the bed that he had difficulty catching his breath. Four other men took hold of Owens' ankles and stood on them as he could feel the cold, hard concrete floor. Out of the corner of his eye, he could see a very large man approaching the bunk. No one spoke; only grunts and groans could be heard from the men holding Owen down. This large, ominous man came from behind the group of men, instructing Owen to stand up and not look at him. The man ripped Owens' shirt open, revealing Mother Mary, and laughed.

"She can't help you now," he said.

Owen continued, saying this man had his way with him. "It was one and done because the man never touched me again, nor did anyone else." Upon the completion of the horrors that took place in his cell that night, the large man said to Owen, "You're one of us now!" Then the gang of inmates turned and walked out. Owen's cellmate then scurried into the cell, unable to make eye contact or say anything. He climbed onto the top bunk, rolled over, and covered his head with the pillow.

Upon finishing his story, Owen and I stared at each other while the awkward silence enveloped the small office until my phone rang and jolted me out of my daze.

"I'm so sorry, I told him." How does one come back from that?"

Owen replied, "You don't, you learn to live with it. The good thing that came from that horrible night was that I was protected from other prison gangs while I was there. I became close with those guys, believe it or not. Being violated had nothing to do with sexual gratification; it was all about power and control."

"What did you miss the most while you were incarcerated?" I quietly asked.

He chuckled as he replied, "Opening doors."

I had a perplexed look on my face. He went on to explain that while he was locked up, everything was done for him, including having doors opened and closed. For the first time in over 4 years, after being paroled early, he was able to open the front gate of the penitentiary and exit on his own. A sense of freedom rushed over him as he left the confines of his temporary home, which was prison.

He went on to say that he no longer takes the act of opening/ closing doors for granted. As silly as it sounds, each time he opens a door and walks through that portal, he is stepping into his new life, a new adventure. He is meeting new friends, spending time with his family, going to work, going to a concert, a movie, and meeting me. Even though Owen was back in the criminal justice world, he said this time it wasn't threatening.

So, the next time you open a door, be mindful of the adventures that await you on the other side of that threshold, no matter how small your journey may be. The simple act of opening a door; how fortuitous, how powerful, how *amazing*!

BEHAVIOR MODIFICATION

People who are placed on probation have not chosen wisely; mistakes have been made, and some of these mistakes are so serious that the law will show its face. Society tries to get their attention by placing them on probation, a.k.a., behavior modification. The maximum amount of time a defendant can spend on misdemeanor probation is up to a 2-year term. Should their misdemeanor probation be messed up, the next step would be a 1-year term in the county jail. While serving as a misdemeanor adult probation officer for 4 years, I can honestly say that 99.9% of the time, the defendants placed on my caseload did not give me any trouble. Defendants wanted to complete probation without incident and contribute to society. My job was to help facilitate that journey.

For felony probation, a defendant can be placed on probation for up to 10 years. Should a defendant violate their felony probation, the punishment was more severe. They went to prison, the gulag, penitentiary, the big house — whatever you wish to call it — for a range of 5 to 99 years. Sadly, several defendants on my caseload found themselves in the big house because they just couldn't or wouldn't handle their time on probation.

JORDAN

JORDAN — 17
Charged with possession of marijuana, less than 2 oz.
Class B misdemeanor
No priors. Given 1-year probation

This was not an unusual offense. I had hundreds of these while I was a misdemeanor officer. I remember him not for his crime but for his *religion.* Jordan was my first satanic follower/worshiper.

Jordan showed up for his first appointment dressed in all black: a black shirt, black pants, and a long black leather jacket. It was June in San Antonio, Texas, and that gave a person cause for pause when someone was wearing a long black leather coat in 100-plus-degree heat. Jordan also donned black painted fingernails, and in the early 90s, young men did not paint their fingernails. Jordan was a respectful, shy young man at first, not offering any personal information that might reveal who he really was. One monthly visit would change all that.

Somehow, religion was brought up in the conversation, and Jordan told me he was a satanic worshiper. He then asked me about my religion, and I told him I was Christian, raised in the Southern Baptist Church. Growing up in West Texas as a Southern Baptist, we were taught, 'love thy neighbor as thyself,' and this was indeed an eye-opener. Jordan explained how he was raised in the occult, stating that his great-grandfather, grandfather, and dad were all leaders in the satanic community. On the next monthly appointment, Jordan brought a satanic book/bible. I immediately raised my hands in protest and didn't touch the book. I asked why he thought it was ok to bring this book into my office.

"You seemed interested, so I thought you might want to read it," he told me.

I kindly declined asking him to remove the book from my desk. Jordan left without issue or insult and went on until our next monthly meeting. Jordan was a good student and was doing well in school. He attended AP classes with the hope of someday attending college to study architecture. Jordan slowly began to shed the black and bring color into his wardrobe. No more punk look, and no more black fingernail polish. His year of probation was coming to an end when he invited me to attend one of the rituals. I asked where they held these. He said it depended on the stars, moon, etc., but it would be held outdoors. I, of course, declined, and he understood. Jordan completed probation satisfactorily, turned eighteen, graduated from high school, and planned to attend a university in another state. I hope he found happiness and success after our time together.

THE BREEDER

MACIE — 22
Charged with failure to identify and resisting arrest
(both class A misdemeanors)
Charged with issuance of a bad check,
Class C misdemeanor.
No priors. Given 2-years probation

Macie had been reporting to me for six months without incident, on time, and had completed her community service hours; at this point, she had completed one of her two court-mandated courses. Macie wasn't working or attending college and skirted the issue each time I asked, "How are you supporting yourself?"

She would respond, "I live with my family, they take care of me."

Until one day, I noticed Macie trying to conceal a bruise on her face by combing her hair over a blue shiner. She also looked pregnant.

I asked her politely, "Macie, are you pregnant?"

Breaking into tears, she replied, "Yes, this is my sixth pregnancy."

I opened her folder to her personal information. "Macie, it says that you have no children, and you're not married."

"The children," she said, breaking into uncontrollable sobs "they aren't mine. I have them, they take them."

"Who are they?" I inquired.

"My family," she responded.

I immediately called my supervisor, who called the FBI and the San Antonio Police Department. We were able to get information from Macie that she was a breeder for a satanic cult. It was discovered that this cult would have rituals wherein they raped young girls and impregnate them. Then they helped them with the births, and then sacrificed the babies during rituals.

The FBI escorted Macie out of my office and out of my life. I never heard from or saw her again. My supervisor told me weeks later that the cult was being investigated, and Macie would get the assistance she needed. That poor girl, I am beyond glad that she decided to trust and confide in me on that day.

WHAT A SHIT SHOW

Before a defendant was called in for their appointment, standard procedure required the assigned probation officer to check the computer to see whether the defendant had an active warrant for their arrest. If they did, a security team member would be waiting in the next office with handcuffs to escort the accused to an office for San Antonio's finest, so SAPD officers could come and take the defendant to jail for processing. A bonus service that we probation officers offered to help apprehend at-large felons and misdemeanants was, of course, without compensation. (You're welcome, SAPD).

Anyhoodle, I digress.

On this particular day, Geller had an appointment with one of her defendants who had an active warrant. Walking into her office, she instructed Mr. Audin to remain standing as Jorge, a security team member, entered.

"Mr. Audin, you have an active warrant," Gellar stated, "and we will be taking you into custody."

As Jorge cuffed Mr. Audin, he retorted, "I think I'm going to be sick."

Mr. Audin proceeded to shit himself. The aroma of feces filled Geller's office and mine, as my office was next to hers. Geller began to gag and asked Jorge to escort Mr. Audin to the restroom to clean up.

We lit candles and sprayed Lysol to no avail, but it still smelled of shit. (I still think of this day when I smell Lysol). It seemed like it took forever to get that smell out of her office. Geller took her appointments down the hall for a few days because of the stench.

Jorge reported to Geller that Mr. Audin tried to clean himself up by turning his underwear inside out before SAPD came to collect and transport him to jail. I am sure it didn't help the situation, if you catch my drift.

It took months before Geller could even laugh or make jokes about this incident. It just goes to show that some days are just shitty... no pun intended.

TITS UP

Geller had a defendant, Carol, a convicted felon for welfare fraud, who had not reported for five months. Numerous attempts to contact Carol via telephone (FYI: pre-cell phone days) were unsuccessful as the defendant's phone number was no longer in service.

Geller also tried visiting Carol on a home visit and found out through a neighbor that she had moved without contacting Geller, her probation officer, which is a big no-no. Five months had passed when Carol just showed up at the department out of the blue to report.

Geller asked, "Where have you been? I've tried contacting you. There is an active warrant for your arrest, citing failure to report for five months, failure to attend your court-mandated classes, and failure to report a change of residence."

Carol immediately stood up and, without any warning, lifted her blouse, revealing her bare breast, showing scars from a recent breast augmentation procedure. Carol began chasing Geller around the tiny office, trying to force her to look at her scars. Geller advised Carol that she needn't show her scars, reminding her that her behavior was inappropriate, and to please take a seat until security could take her into custody.

A few days later, at Carol's motion to revoke hearing, the judge was advised of the revocation violations, including the most recent inappropriate breast exposure. I wasn't present, but I heard that Judge had to hide his/her smirk, probably picturing Geller being chased by the defendant in her small office. Instead of backing the officer, the judge laughed it off and kept the defendant on probation without any punishment. For years, Judge would see Geller and tease her about the boob incident. Geller eventually laughed about it, and it gave us yet another story to tell.

ONLY THE NOSE KNOWS

Geller's office was next to mine, so hearing almost everything that happened in her office was not unusual, just as she could hear almost everything that was said in mine. Remember, due to "security" reasons, or so we were told, our offices were void of doors. (Interesting fact: all of the offices in the newer buildings now have doors.) So, one day, I heard Geller gasp as a male defendant entered her office.

"Mr. Edgars, where is your nose?" she asked.

What in the world was she speaking of, I wondered, so of course, I had to investigate. I got up from my office chair and took the ten steps into the hall over to Geller's doorway. She had a look of disgust on her face and her hand over her mouth as if she was going to lose her lunch.

Mr. Edgars replied, "I left my nose in the cab."

Geller advised Mr. Edgars that she would not see him until he had recovered his nose. Geller showed Mr. Edgars out of her office, reminding him that he is never ever allowed to report without his nose affixed to his face. As Mr. Edgars turned to leave the office, his face revealed pinkish muscle tissue and a bone in the center of his nose, something out of a horror movie. Quite frankly, I am sure I gasped out loud as well, not a proud moment, but I was caught by surprise.

Curious, aren't you? Here is how Mr. Edgars lost his nose.

Sadly, years earlier, Mr. Edgars was attempting to take his own life. He had a gun in his mouth when he discharged the weapon, and the gun recoiled, shooting up into his nose. Mr. Edgars survived and had facial surgery. The plastic surgeon was able to make a prosthetic nose for Mr. Edgars to wear.

I have no idea why the nose was not permanently attached, but it wasn't. It was traveling in the back of a San Antonio cab, and I feel bad for the poor soul who was the next occupant of that cab!

Rest assured, a month later, Mr. Edgars was reunited with his nose! Geller saw Mr. Edgars at his next report, with his nose in its proper place.

BLIND MAN'S BLUFF

County Court at Law No. 9 had the dubious honor of being large and in charge of *all* misdemeanor domestic violence cases, as well as many other misdemeanor crimes. The remaining misdemeanor courts were relieved that our judge had tasked us, the probation officers, with these cases, as they were arduous, exhausting, and time-consuming. This is one of the reasons the CC #9 had twice as many officers in the court.

As I mentioned earlier, our caseloads were in the upper three hundreds, while other officers in other courts maintained a much lower caseload, in the mid- to high- hundreds. Financial compensation was not in the equation; we were paid the same as all the other officers, even though we had three times as much work.

Geller had a man assigned to her caseload who had beaten his wife substantially, leaving her badly bruised with a broken rib, which was not unusual for our cases, but this man was blind.

Each month when Mr. Jones reported, Geller would escort the defendant via the elevator from the first-floor waiting room to the second floor, where our offices were located. Mr. Jones maneuvered the halls with a walking stick, holding on to Geller's arm for added support, and wore very dark sunglasses. Mr. Jones reported to her each month without incident. He had reconciled with his wife, attended counseling, and was performing community service.

On this particular day, just after Geller completed her appointment with Mr. Jones, she and a few of us went to our break in front of the probation department building. I happened to notice Mr. Jones walking down the street without his dark sunglasses. As he approached a car, he threw his walking stick onto the back of a four-door Honda Accord and got into the driver's seat. He started the car and drove right past us, not seeing that we were standing there with our mouths wide open.

"Geller, isn't that Mr. Jones?" I asked.

"Yep, it sure is!"

I laughed as I said, "I was always curious why his wife wasn't able to get away from him. A blind man beating his wife, how is that possible?"

Geller extinguished her cigarette on the hot concrete and rushed into the building, bounding up the stairs, taking two steps at a time. Geller prepared a motion to revoke Mr. Jone's probation since he has lied to her. The next day, the judge was presented with the motion but simply laughed it off, telling Geller to continue Mr. Jone's probation, as he would only be on her caseload for a few more months.

The following month, Mr. Jones reports as scheduled, as Geller advised him to take the elevator up on his own, stating there was no escort for him that day. His charade continued as he wore his dark sunglasses and used the walking stick to enter Geller's office. I remember Geller telling Mr. Jones that his lies about being blind had been discovered and that numerous witnesses, including herself, had seen him drive off after his last appointment. He had the nerve to say that she must have been mistaken because he was indeed blind and she must have seen someone who looked like him.

As Mr. Jones was leaving, Geller stood to watch him exit her office and proceed down the hall. What she did next was clever.

"Mr. Jones, is that your $20 bill on the floor?" she asked.

He quickly turned around, removing his dark sunglasses from his head, and looked down at the ground. He then looked up to see Geller glaring at him as she revealed his lie. As she turned to enter her office from the hall, she said, "See you next month, Mr. Jones."

THERE'S NO PLACE LIKE HOME

STEVEN — 18
Charged with possession of 2–4 oz. of marijuana
No priors. Given 2-years probation
(High school senior. C-average. Smokes with friends)

Steven was not the brightest star in the sky, but a respectful young man. He reported each month but refused to begin his court-mandated drug awareness classes, nor had he started working on community service hours. His mother, a single working mom, was deeply concerned for her son, as she had seen a decline in Steven's behavior: failing grades, breaking curfew, and spending time with people she didn't like. Bless her heart, she would ring me up weekly seeking advice on what she should do. I sympathized with her, made suggestions, but sadly, the behavior did not improve.

I began seeing Steven every week instead of once a month, hoping to get his attention. He knew he was heading down a rabbit hole that he may not be able to get out of. I encouraged him to get a job and work a few hours after school and on weekends. I helped him secure a job at a movie theatre, which helped the situation. Steven was working 20 hours a week, saving his hard-earned money, focusing more on school as his grades improved, and expressed interest in joining the military after graduating high school. I was happy, his mom was happy, but most importantly, Steven was happy. Another success story.

Months passed, and I had Steven return to monthly reporting. His community service hours were completed, the drug awareness class was finished, school was good, and his job at the theater was going well. As part of my job, I was to conduct random drug tests on defendants assigned to my caseload. On this day, I called Steven before he went to school, advising him that I needed to perform a drug test on him. I instructed him to report to my office as soon as he finished his last class. It would only take ten minutes, and he could be home by 5:00 pm.

"Sure, Ms. Moody, I will be there right after school, have a good day."

"You too, Steven. See you this afternoon."

Around 4:00 that afternoon, security from downstairs notified me that Steven was there for his report.

"Ms. Moody, Steven is here, but he doesn't look so good," Evie, the security monitor, told me.

I called him to my office immediately. I remember standing at the end of my long hall, watching Steven come towards me. I smelled a strong bleach odor. He approached my office, eyes dark, and he was having difficulty walking. Steven barely made it through the door when he collapsed on the chair.

"Ms. Moody, I'm here for my ddrurggg tsssst," he said in slurred speech.

"Steven, did you drink bleach?" I asked.

His eyes rolled back in his head, and he threw up. I yelled for help and called 911 from my office phone. Steven was convulsing on my floor. Security came and tried to render aid. EMS arrived within minutes, placed Steven on a gurney, and whisked him off to Santa Rosa Hospital, just around the corner from our building. I called Steven's mother and advised her that her son had been taken to the hospital, and she needed to get down there as quickly as possible.

Shaking and crying, I tried to clean up my office. The small room reeked of bleach. What just happened? A colleague took my last report so I could go to the hospital. When I arrived at the ER, I was unable to get anyone to tell me how Steven was doing, as I wasn't the next of kin. Steven's mother arrived at the hospital within the hour. She looked around the crowded and bustling ER and approached me, asking if I was Ms. Moody. I told her yes, and she fell into my arms, crying. We had never met face to face, but we held onto each other as if we had known each other our whole lives. We made our way to the nurse's station, hoping to get information about her son.

Thirty minutes later, a doctor emerged from the back of the ER informing Steven's mom that her son didn't make it. The consumption of bleach didn't allow his kidneys to process the toxins, causing him to go into renal failure. *What???* I had never witnessed anyone dying in person. He was so young, and his death was so senseless. Had I been responsible for this young man's death? What if I hadn't made the call to have him report, to take the drug test? What if, what if, what if? Only 18-years-old. He was doing so well, and it was just marijuana. *Why?*

I made sure Steven's mom was not alone before I left the hospital. Her sister arrived to help her get a handle on what this poor woman's new normal would be. My supervisor met me as I was exiting the hospital, and asked if I was ok.

"What am I supposed to do with all this?" I cried.

The guilt I felt was overwhelming. I was instructed to take the rest of the week off, seek professional help/therapy, and take some time. Time? Time was my enemy; too much time to repeatedly reimagine the recent events. I couldn't sit at home and handle this on my own, so I went home to my parents, Bob and Charlotte, who were 7 hours away in Lubbock, Texas. I didn't even go to my apartment to pack clothes. I just got into my car and drove to my safe place, my childhood home.

Mom and Dad were waiting up for me when I arrived around 3:00 a.m. I don't remember the long dark drive. I just drove, cried, and drove some more. I fell asleep crying in my parents' king-sized bed, awaking to our miniature dachshund, Fritz, licking my face and wagging his tail. Dad was asleep on my right; Mom was on my left, and she was still hugging me.

Dad woke up and went to the kitchen to make coffee, and I went to take a much-needed hot shower. Mom was making breakfast, Dad poured coffee into three mugs, and no one said a word. At one point, before we converged at the breakfast table, we embraced in a family hug in the middle of the kitchen. We grabbed our coffee mugs and sat at the round table. Dad was reading the Avalanche Journal, possibly the worst newspaper ever published, while Mom set a beautiful plated feast: a cheese omelet, sausage links, a watermelon slice, and a cup of strawberries and blueberries. Dad answered the kitchen phone and told Patti, his assistant, that he would be in that morning, but to please ask Philip to handle the deposition scheduled for this afternoon.

"Pam has come home," he told her. "I'm going to take her and Charlotte down to the ranch for a few days. I will tell you the details later."

Dad came to the breakfast table where I was seated, kissed me on the forehead, and looked me in the eyes. "You're going to be all right. Take a deep breath, cry, do whatever you need to. You will get on the other side of this. I will be home around noon, and we will head out to Slaton."

"Ok, Dad, that sounds great."

Dad showered, dressed for the office, and off he went. Mom and I left the dirty dishes in the sink, took our coffee to the sunroom, sat on the couch, where Mom listened to me talk, cry, talk, and then talk some more.

My dad had been an attorney for over 40 years at this point. He was an estate, oil and gas, and ranching lawyer who also represented large companies. He loved being a lawyer. When he introduced himself to strangers, he would say, "Bob Moody, lawyer from Lubbock, Texas, how are you doing?"

Both of my parents were sixth-generation Texans and very proud of that fact. My mom's family was one of the first 100 families to settle in Texas. She was also a member of the Daughters of the Republic of Texas. One of my mom's descendants perished in the battle at the Alamo in San Antonio. My sister, Leigh, and I were not allowed to be in these elite organizations. We were adopted and weren't from the bloodline, so membership in either group was prohibited.

Spending a week with my parents grounded me. Dad was always the voice of reason, dishing out solid and sound wisdom, while Mom just held me, listened, and let me cry. Fritz never left my side. He lay in my lap and slept with me. He knew I needed him, and he delivered.

I returned to work after a week. I went back to my job guarded and with reservations. A month had passed since Steven's death. I was unable to attend his funeral because I was at my folks', so I asked his mother if I could visit her. She was surprised when I called, and she invited me to her home, where I was welcomed with open arms. I was met with assurances by Steven's mom that he was the one who chose to drink the bleach in hopes of masking his recent marijuana usage. I left Steven's mom with a heartfelt hug, letting her know what a great young man her son was, and how proud I was of his diligence and achievements while he was on my caseload. I told her that she should also be proud of the respectful and kind person that she had raised.

I ran into Steven's mom at a high school graduation many years later. She recognized me in the crowd, approached with a smile, and asked if I remembered her.

"Yes!!! Of course, how are you?" I asked.

She introduced me to her nephew, the graduate, and her family, telling them I was Steven's probation officer and that I was great with him. We hugged, looking at her nephew. "Congratulations on your graduation," I told him.

Steven's mom and I locked eyes, and we both began to tear up a little. She smiled and grabbed my hand with a tender squeeze, then walked away into the crowd with her family.

My guilt over this young man's death still haunts me 30 years later, and I still ask myself *what if?* I remember my dad's words, "You will get on the other side of this," and hopefully, someday I will.

It isn't often that a defendant on one's caseload dies during their probation terms, but it does happen, unfortunately. It happened to me twice. Two times too many.

AARON — 22
Charged with driving while intoxicated, a class B misdemeanor.
No priors. Given 2-years probation.

Aaron was a full-time student at the University of Texas at San Antonio (UTSA), studying business. He worked weekends at a local bar near the university, and he lived at home with his parents, saving money to move out after graduation. UTSA wasn't the size it is today, and the area where the university is located off the 1604 highway wasn't the four-lane mega monster it is today. The 1604 was called the death loop because of the fatalities that happened on that part of the road. It was only two lanes and had no night illumination.

Aaron was an uncooperative defendant assigned to my caseload. He was disrespectful, didn't report on time, hadn't begun his mandated court classes, and hadn't started working on his 100 hours of community service. He was the kind of person who always had excuses: "It wasn't my fault," "I didn't do it." "I wasn't that drunk." "I don't belong here." "I'm not a criminal like the rest of those guys sitting in the waiting room." He never took responsibility for his actions, which made my job even more difficult. He was exhausting to deal with, and I didn't look forward to our monthly meetings.

Sunday morning activities in our household included numerous pots of hot coffee, waffles with warm Vermont maple syrup, and snuggles on the couch. Reading the San Antonio Express-News was a part of that ritual. It was six months into Aaron's probation at this time, which would be the end of our time together. After work Saturday evening, Aaron decided to get intoxicated and speed on 1604. He drove off an overpass at 120 miles per hour onto the highway below, ending up upside down.

Aaron died in that crash, as well as his girlfriend and his girlfriend's roommate. The headline read, "UTSA Students Killed in Rollover," and it gave me a queasy feeling while reading the paper. I felt it in my gut. You know that feeling you get when you think something is wrong, terribly wrong? Aaron's name and that of his friends had not been printed in the newspaper, since the two girls' parents had not been notified yet of their daughters' deaths. My intuitions were validated on Monday morning when I received a call at my office from Aaron's mom advising me that he had been killed in a car crash.

I would come to find out later that Aaron's blood alcohol content was 3.8, and the two girls had no alcohol or any illegal substances in their systems at the time of the crash. Why hadn't one of the girls driven? Why did they get into the car knowing Aaron was drunk? Why did he drive drunk, speed, and then fly off the overpass, taking two innocent people with him? Oh, I guess because *it wasn't his fault, he wasn't that drunk.*

Three people died that night, and their deaths were so senseless. Aaron was a difficult defendant. I just wish he had taken probation more seriously because maybe he and his friends would still be alive today.

KARMA'S A BITCH

Monday morning docket call, seated in the courtroom, patiently awaiting the judge to begin our weekly routine of motions and pleas. Another week of court, another week of the same old, same old, but suddenly a youngish woman in her early 30s walked into the misdemeanor courtroom for her case: driving while intoxicated, second offense.

She was dressed to the nines in beautiful clothes, high heels, manicured nails, a recently coiffed hairdo, and in tow was her high-dollar attorney. Flinging her Louis Vuitton handbag about, not paying any attention as she smacked a man in the face with her Louis. She plopped herself down, with no apologies to the recently shocked man she had just accosted. You could tell this woman felt as if she was too good to be there. How dare the judicial system waste her time by having her come downtown to the courthouse? She had things to do. She kept looking at her watch, griping to her attorney, asking what was taking so long.

I'm sure she was in a hurry to make her weekly luncheon at the San Antonio Country Club with all her buffy and biffy friends. I enjoyed watching this play out, and I couldn't wait to make eye contact with this person.

A few minutes passed, and the Bailiff announced, "All rise, the honorable Judge Rogers presiding."

She stood, rolling her eyes and looking at her watch as the judge instructed the courtroom, "Please be seated."

The woman saw me, and her eyes grew wide as she placed her hand over her mouth in shock. Her attitude became visibly different.

We recognized each other. Penelope, or Pen, as her close friends and family called her. This woman was one of the original *mean girls* of our high school, in dusty, tumbleweed-laden Lubbock, Texas. The movie was probably written with dear ole Pen in mind.

On one occasion, Penelope purposely tripped a good friend of mine while she was walking down the hall at school, breaking this girl's nose and chipping two teeth, sending her to the oral surgeon. Pen also keyed her English teacher's car because she received a failing grade. I heard no punishment was given to Pen for this act. She was your typical spoiled rotten to the core kind of girl. Pen had her daddy wrapped around her finger, and daddy didn't dish out consequences, allowing her to do whatever the hell she wanted.

Each year, Pen was given a new car. In her senior year, Daddy gave her a 1956 vintage two-seater T-bird. I hear she pitched a fit because it wasn't a brand-new car. What a bitch. I was just grateful to have a car, and I shared an orange and white AMC Gremlin with my little sister. Our gremlin was void of power steering but adorned with the orange Levi brand label, as the seats were made of Levi denim. It was also loaded with an eight-track player. Talk about vintage, I wish I had that car today.

Anyhoo... Pen and I went to high school together. When I was a sophomore, she was a senior. Her boyfriend at the time asked me out on a date, and they ended up breaking up over it. Let it be known that I did not accept the advances, as my folks thought I was too young to date. Upon graduating from Coronado High School in Lubbock, Texas, Pen attended and graduated from The University of Texas in Austin, where she met and married a San Antonio boy, thus ending up in the same town, which I now call home. Small world, not small enough.

Finally, Pen's name was called, and it was her turn to face the music for her *second DWI*. As Pen approached the bench with her attorney, she turned her ankle on her high heels. Thankfully, her attorney caught her. I have to say, I was enjoying this a bit too much. I didn't take my eyes off her; I glared her down, and she knew it. Beads of sweat were forming on her brow, and she was so nervous that she stammered over her words when the judge asked her questions.

Finally, the morning docket was complete, and it was now my turn to interview the defendants. I immediately grabbed Pen's folder before the other officers could retrieve it. I purposely made her wait, and she was the very last person to be interviewed. I know it wasn't a Christian thing to do, but oh, it sure felt good to have this much power over Pen.

I called her into the small conference room located outside the courtroom and motioned for her to take a seat across from me at the large table. She sat down and gingerly placed her Louis in a chair beside her.

"So, I bet you're just loving this?" she sarcastically asked me.

Inside my sick little head, I wanted to slap her with her heavy purse, knocking her out of kingdom come and back, but my response was very professional. "What do you mean?"

"You know exactly what I mean," Pen responded as she nervously adjusted in her chair.

"Pen, that was years ago, that's all water under the bridge."

What sweet, stupid, mean, unassuming Pen didn't realize was that I was about to make her life just a little more miserable than it had to be. As a probation officer, I had the authority to assign her an extra class, which I did.

I also increased her community service hours from 50 to 100. Plus, I assigned her community service hours so she would be collecting trash along the sides of highways. This would require good ol' Pen to be outdoors, and she would have to wear a huge yellow vest donning the words, *PROBATIONER AT WORK*. (That one was my favorite!). I also increased her alcoholics anonymous (AA) meetings from once a week to twice a week. She also had to report in person four times a month instead of once a month for the first six months of her probation. All these things would benefit Pen, not hurt her, but it was a major inconvenience.

Pen whispered, "Are you going to be my PO?"

"No, Pen, since we know each other, it would be a conflict of interest. I will be seeing you around the office, though."

She signed her conditions of probation and sprinted out of the conference room as quickly as her high heels would allow. I did see Pen around the office occasionally, and I was always pleasant and professional. Pen barely made it through her 2-year stint with probation. Apparently, dear sweet Pen had a bit of a drinking problem and wasn't willing to get a handle on it.

A few years later, my mom sent me a newspaper clipping from the Lubbock Avalanche Journal. It was Pen's obituary; she had died from liver disease. I know this sounds mean, but I guess that saying is true... Karma really is a bitch!

WIZZ-A-NATOR 2000

I love sharing this story. It's both humorous and educational. One of the many tasks that must be performed by adult probation officers is ensuring the safety and sobriety of the probationers on our caseloads, so drug tests are conducted as mandated by the courts. Tests can be performed weekly or biweekly, but they are typically random. The drug test consists of the collection of urine/pee, in lieu of blood or hair follicles, which is more economical and easier to obtain.

Four male technicians, dumb and dumber times two, ran the drug lab, which was housed in one of the three buildings that we worked in. The four male technicians would observe the male probationers pee into a thermal sterilized cup, and the female adult probation officers would observe the female probationers pee into a thermal sterilized cup. Did you pick up on that little fact?

To save a buck, Chief refused to hire female technicians, so we female officers had to observe our probationers peeing in a cup. Not only awkward but ewwww. This was not a task we female officers relished, but yet another machismo act against the female population at Bexar County Adult Probation.

Let me describe in DETAIL how the urine/pee is collected for drug tests: The law stipulates that a person of authority, technician, probation officer, test administrator, etc., *must* witness the urine/pee exiting the body of the probationer. This is called the *chain of custody*. The collector/observer will then feel/handle the cup, of course, with gloves on. The urine sample should be warm to the touch, because, as we all know, science 101, urine/pee should be warm when it exits the human body. The urine sample will then be taken to the lab, where one of the four lab technicians will test it for illegal substances. Should a probationer test positive for an illegal substance or substances, the probation officer would then be notified. The officer is then required to file a motion to revoke probation with the court. At some point, the probationer will have to answer the judge as to why they did indeed test positive for drugs.

The officers will have to testify: "Yes, your honor, I did indeed observe the pee/urine exit the probationer's body on this date at this time, had it tested at our lab, positive results occurred, and that is why we are in front of you today, Your honor."

It was on rare occasions that a probationer would go to prison based on a positive drug test. It usually just meant that more drug treatment or drug rehabilitation courses were offered to the probationer.

The probationer I'm describing next was not on my caseload, but I think you will enjoy the facts of this case. A male lab technician was observing three men pee into a cup for a drug test. The technician noticed that the coloration of one of the male appendages (a.k.a. penis) did not match that of the rest of his body. Do you follow? Hmmmm, interesting. The touch test revealed the sample is cold to the touch; even more interesting.

The lab technician informed the probationer's probation officer of the situation, and the officer responded by having the probationer submit another test. This time, the probationer would be observed providing another urine sample in the presence of the probation officer and two lab technicians. These three would witness not only the emergence of one penis but two penises escaping from the probationer's pants. The probationer had a fake penis holding a urine sample known as the *Wizz-a-Nator 2000*. These can be purchased at head shops and nowadays online for drug tests.

The newest urine sample was tested, revealing positive results for heroin, marijuana, and meth. The probation officer contacted the court to ask for further instructions. The judge wished to see the probationer, the probation officer, and the two lab technicians who witnessed the chain of custody. Oh, he also wanted to see the *Wizz-a-Nator 2000*.

I was not in the courtroom, but I heard these were the events as they unfolded. The judge summoned the bailiff, court reporter, the prosecutor, the probationer's attorney of record, and, of course, the probationer. They all approached the bench; the court reporter was typing everything that was said to record the recent events for the court record. The lab technicians testified in the order in which it occurred; the probation officer was also put on the stand to testify about his role in this most recent drug test. Then the judge asked the probationer to take the stand, and asked him where he got the *Wizz-a-Nator*. The probationer's reply was that he had purchased it at a local head shop. The judge apparently was amused as he held up the evidence bag containing the latex penis. By this time, onlookers and bailiffs from other courts were now positioned, standing room only, to hear as the *Wizz-a-Nator* was entered into evidence as Exhibit A.

I heard there were several giggles in the courtroom. The judge apparently had a smirk on his face as he slowly turned toward the probationer. "Where did you acquire the urine for today's drug test, sir?" the judge asked.

The probationer apparently also had a smirk on his face as he replied, "My baby."

I guess the judge went from smiling to astonished disgust within a second and a half. His face reportedly turned three shades of red, and he almost popped a blood vessel pulsing from the middle of his forehead. The judge then looked at the probationer's court record, which I can tell you is not stellar. This young man, a new dad, unemployed, drug-using a-hole, was sentenced to 25 years in prison. I was told it took four bailiffs to escort him to the holding cell. There wasn't a smirk on anybody's face after that judgment.

The probation officer and the two lab technicians returned to the drug lab, victorious with the *Wizz-a-Nator 2000* secured tightly in the evidence bag. It would be displayed proudly on the bulletin board for all to see, and what a sight it was. Judges came from the courthouse to see this thing, the same judges who had never taken the time or energy to enter our little condemned office building with the broken furniture. The *Wizz-a-Nator 2000* would be the catalyst to get them out of the world of the forgotten and overlooked.

TOMATO *TOMATOE...*
A NAME IS JUST A NAME

I was employed by the Bexar County Adult Probation Department in 1990 as a misdemeanor probation officer. That meant something to me, and I was proud to be a part of this profession. At the time, approximately 3,000 probation officers were employed across the entire state of Texas. It is, after all, an unusual profession to be in. How many probation officers do you know?

It meant huge responsibilities, and I was empowered to help protect the citizens of San Antonio, Texas, the community that I had chosen to call home. It also meant that I would be able to help individuals who had committed some horrible crimes, as well as help them repair their families, which were adjusting to the mistakes made by their loved ones. People who break the law involve not just the victim. The community is also impacted; the victim's family and friends, their neighbors, the defendant's family and friends, their neighbors, the victims' pets, the defendant's pets, and even the people who work in the court system. Judges, bailiffs, court reporters, prosecutors, defense attorneys, court clerks, court coordinators, jurors, and probation officers can all be affected by this ripple.

I can't even begin to tell you how many times I cried on my drive home from a long day in court after a defendant on my caseload was sentenced to prison. Yes, they deserved to go to prison, but when families are in the courtroom hearing their loved ones being sentenced to prison time or even given the death penalty, there is cause for pause. How many more lives are interrupted and disrupted by one person's acts?

In 1993, the 71st Texas Legislature enacted a change in the law:

The term "probation officer" was officially changed to "community supervision officer." Probation and community supervision officer is now considered interchangeable. It is said that the reason for the change is "to reflect a broader focus on offender rehabilitation and reintegration into the community, rather than solely focusing on punishment, signifying that the role involves actively supervising individuals within the community as an alternative to incarceration." (1993, 71st Texas Legislation).

I remember the day this occurred; I was upset by this change. You see, I had been hired to be a tough, but fair, probation officer, an officer of the court. But now the great state of Texas was asking me to be a community supervision officer. It just lost its umph, its meat, its zeal. Let me ask you this, as a reader, if you're at a cocktail party and you meet an adult probation officer, you want to talk to that person, right? They have interesting stories from the people they encounter to the things they see and hear. It's just not your average, every day, run-of-the-mill stuff. But a community supervision officer? Yeah, I'm thinking not. Instead, you would be headed over to the bar to get another gin and tonic. We bitches of Bexar County never embraced the title "community supervision officer." We were and forever will be PROBATION OFFICERS, because a name *isn't* just a name.

THE FELONY FOLLIES

Double-Secret Probation
(a.k.a. ISP – Intensive Supervision Probation)

My four years assigned to the misdemeanor court would pass quickly. Wanting a new challenge, I applied and was promoted to a felony court. I received a small raise and was relocated to a new building. My new digs had a view of the San Antonio River, and the office was a *real* office with carpeting and even a door. Yep, I had a door to open and close, which may not sound like a big deal, but let me assure you, it was. My caseload was no longer 400 people; it was now 35. That's right, only 35 felons whom I would be responsible for. Although the caseload had declined, the crimes had not.

Murder, aggravated sexual assault (a.k.a. rape), arson, attempted capital murder, injury to a child, trafficking of persons, aggravated kidnapping (a.k.a. use of a weapon was involved while kidnapping an individual), indecency of a child, intoxication manslaughter, robbery, burglary of a habitation, and arson. The list goes on.

The reason my caseload was so limited is that these defendants were placed on what I call double-secret *probation*. Translation: the probationer had failed to meet the mandated conditions set by the court, so the felony judges were willing to give these individuals *one* last chance to straighten out their lives or face prison. Those prison terms ranged from 5 to 99 years. The individuals assigned to me would have to be seen in person at least twice a week, and some were seen daily. Drug and alcohol tests would be performed at each visit instead of random testing, and additional treatment had to be completed by the defendants along with their community service.

Each defendant knew they had to walk a tight rope and not make any mistakes, or their next home would be provided by the great state of Texas, known as prison. The pressure was on! Not just for me, but for the probationer as well. As adult probation officers, we were viewed as *Protectors of Society*, a huge responsibility we did not take lightly. We did not want to be in the newspapers or on the nightly news for not doing our jobs. Remember, we were already considered "the red-headed stepchildren," so bad press would not help our cause.

FROM FOUR WALLS
TO SHOWER STALLS

Nirvana in my office space would be short-lived. Sadly, the ISP probation officers and offices were relocated to another building, which was a renovated jail facility. My office didn't have walls that reached the ceiling, because it had been a former shower. You read correctly: a tile-laden, slanted floor, a drain in the middle of the room, and a shower. The faucets, shower heads, and towel bars had been removed, of course. The area was so small that I had to stand outside my office to change my mind. My office desk and office chair barely fit. When a defendant reported, I would have to slide a chair in from outside the shower stall and have them sit in the door opening. Definitely not safe, should I need to make a quick getaway.

This situation really made me feel like a stepchild in the department, and my new promotion felt like a demotion. The only benefit of being in this building was that the drug lab was just down the hall, making it easier to escort defendants to their drug tests. This is where I would remain for the duration of my time as an officer with the Bexar County Adult Probation Department. There must be some symbolism in that, I just don't know what it is.

THE COLOR BROWN

EVAN — 18
Charged with arson, first offense felony
No priors. Given 2-years probation

Have you ever encountered someone who just isn't there? Glazed over, slouchy, disheveled, moody, grumpy, and plain old disrespectful; this would be one of my first experiences as a felony officer.

Not to be indelicate, but Evan's elevator not only didn't go to the top floor, but it also never opened. Evan was late for his first appointment—no surprise there. He became agitated when I questioned him about his tardiness, proclaiming it was none of my 'beeswax' as to why he was late. This young man would push every one of my buttons while trying my patience, and, to top it off, I got to see him every day.

Evan had dropped out of school in the tenth grade, wasn't employed, had no friends, no hobbies, and lived with his parents in a trailer out in the middle of nowhere. You get the picture. He was placed on my caseload because he hadn't accomplished anything under his former felony probation officer, so the judge placed him in ISP with me. Yay!!! Protocol dictated that a daily drug test be performed on Evan.

I would have bet my measly paycheck that he was under the influence of drugs, but all his test results would reveal that he was clean and didn't use any illegal substances. He just didn't care about anything. He was what we call *ODD* in the biz: oppositional defiance disorder. My first experience with this disorder was not only extremely frustrating but also fascinating. I could never understand if he didn't care about anything, then why would he report to probation? He cared enough to show up each day, and he cared enough to submit to his daily drug test, but he refused to gain employment, and he refused to begin his court-mandated programs or perform any of his community service.

Evan's crime was arson, and the facts of the case are as follows: A Texas state trooper was driving on the highway when he noticed black smoke coming from a field. The trooper investigated when he encountered Evan standing very close to a burning SUV. Next to Evan's feet was an empty gas can and a box of matches. The trooper notified the local volunteer fire department to extinguish the fire, and no one was hurt, except the SUV. The trooper testified in court that when he asked the defendant why he was standing in the field with a gas can and matches, Evan simply stated, "My uncle didn't like this SUV. He just bought it and asked me to blaze it up so he could get a new one. Promised me $500 in cash if I did it, so I did."

Billy Bob, Evan's uncle, stated in court that he did not ask his nephew, Evan, to burn his car; he just took it upon himself to blaze the car. The jury found Evan guilty and placed him on probation. One fact that I find interesting is that Billy Bob, Evan's uncle, drove him to his probation appointment every day. I chalk it up to guilt; I'm just saying. Three months passed, and Evan was still not engaging. I took Evan back in front of the judge for a progress report, or rather lack of a progress report, in this case, seeking guidance from the court. The judge was equally as frustrated as I was. What was going on with this young man?

I suggested to the court that I would make a home visit, get a better sense of what we were dealing with, and report back to the court. Judge agreed, so early one weekday morning, I *volun-told* a friend, another officer, that we were going on a *field trip* to Evan's family home. I had attempted to get in touch with Evan's folks to let them know we would be out for a home visit, but they had no phones.

The drive seemed long, especially since I had never been to this part of Bexar County. We drove off the highway and onto a bumpy farm-to-market road, which had not been paved yet. It was a mild November day. The air was crisp and cool, the sun was hidden behind clouds, and a foggy mist rose from the fields, giving the impression that we were driving into a black-and-white watercolor. I was playing a cassette tape of Earth, Wind & Fire, as we drove onto Evan's family's property. Dismal doesn't begin to describe what we were looking at.

Exiting the car, we were greeted by numerous free-range chickens, three friendly dogs, and, under the trailer home, newborn kittens with their momma. The trailer didn't have a door, just a heavy blanket to keep the elements out. An old, beat-up Chevy with missing tires was on the back side of the trailer. We could hear the daily news being broadcast as we walked up the rickety steps, trying to locate a place to knock on to announce our arrival.

My partner loudly announced, "HELLO, hello, good morning, we're with the adult probation office. We're here to see the James family."

The TV was so loud, I was surprised to see the blanket move, revealing a man who looked like something out of the movie *Deliverance*. I gasped as my partner kept me from falling off the steps that we were both occupying, wearing our fancy high heels.

"Is you lost? What do you want?"

"Sir, we're here to see Evan…"

"Evan? Why?"

I retrieved my probation badge from my coat pocket, showed it to Mr. James, and handed him my business card.

"May we come in?"

Mrs. James rescued us from Mr. James, nudging him aside.

"You come on into this house, c'mon!"

The trailer was warm, as the blanket seemed to keep the cold air at bay. The home's interior did not disappoint either; it was equally scary as the exterior. The shag carpet was brown, the furniture was brown, the walls were brown paneling, and the linoleum in the kitchen was brown. Everything was brown.

"Can I offer you yung'un's some coffee?" she asked.

"No ma'am, thank you though. We don't want to take up too much of your time. We just wanted to introduce ourselves and visit Evan. Is he available?"

Mrs. James stated that Evan was out hunting for breakfast.

"Hunting? With a gun?" I asked.

She laughed and replied, "How else do you get a squirrel?'

I looked at my partner with wide eyes and said, "Mrs. James, Evan is on felony probation, which means he's not allowed to be around, own, or shoot any guns."

"Oh." Mrs. James became agitated. "How is *we* to know dat?" she exclaimed.

I agreed, "Yes ma'am, you're right, how would you know that?"

Mrs. James waddled off to the kitchen, ignoring our denial of the morning's brew, and she began to pour coffee into three brown mugs. Not wanting to dare upset Mrs. James further, I accepted the coffee.

"Thank you so much, Mrs. James. It smells delicious."

"Cream, sugah?"

"No ma'am, this is perfect," I told her, pretending to sip the god-only-knows-what was in those cups, while trying to make small talk with Mrs. James.

My partner, wandering to the side of the couch, made eye contact with me, looking down at a large patch of carpet that had been cut out, exposing the bare floor below. The naked floor extended by the couch and down the hallway, and you couldn't help but notice it. Mrs. James saw that we were curious and began walking over to the patch.

"Yeah, we're aimin' on new carpenten, what color ew think we should get?

"I like blue, it goes well with brown," I told her.

Without making any noise, Mrs. James nodded her head in agreement. Whew, that was a close one.

A few odd moments passed when Evan entered through the back door of the trailer, toting three squirrels. He nervously bellowed, "Why they here?'

"Morning, Evan," I said. "We're required to perform home visits on all defendants, so here we are."

I was more nervous than he was, but hopefully only my partner was able to pick up on this fact. Evan retrieved a glass from the brown kitchen cabinet, opened the refrigerator, poured himself a large glass of chocolate milk, and then sat on the couch. "Well, do we talk or what?" he asked.

Mrs. James reminded Evan of his manners and sat next to him, placing her hand on his knee. Mrs. James then instructed Mr. James to turn the television off and go outside. He grumbled, then grabbed a jacket and headed out through the front "blanket." Evan sank into the couch, my partner was still positioned over the bare patch on the floor, while I stood in the middle of the room, my left knee hitting the brown wooden coffee table. The air in the room became still and quiet.

Mrs. James began to speak. "Bet you're wondering what happened there?" She asked, pointing to the big uncarpeted patch of the floor. She took a deep, purposeful breath and continued. "Bout three years ago, Mr. James, Evan, and I came home from the fall fair. Evan's brother, Vinny, and Vin's girl was here. We heard screams so we was running to see what was goin on. Evan saw first, it ain't good. Vinny was having relations with his girl, and she didn't care too much for what was hap'n to her, so she was screamin. Screamin like you'd never heard. Vinny, well, he well…he slit her throat, and she was crying and making horrible noise. Vin got evn' more upset, so he stabbed her, over and over until she wuldn't scream no more."

Mrs. James begins to cry. I swallowed hard and was paralyzed. My partner didn't move either, as she was fixated on Mrs. James next words.

"Evan tried to stop Vinny, but there was no stoppin that boy once he got mad. Evan saw tings a 15-year-old boy shouldn't see. He looked up to Vin, you know?" Mrs. James continued, "Evan coundn't go nowhere after that, school, church, nowhere."

She lovingly squeezed Evan's knee. Evan just sat there, showing no emotion.

After a long pause, Mrs. James took a deep breath, "Vin, he's over there in Huntsville on death row."

I heard myself gasp.

"We ain't been over to see him, jus too dif cult."

"Mrs. James, I am so sorry," I told her, and walked towards the couch to extend my hand.

Mrs. James shrugged me off, not in a rude way, but in a way that she didn't want to bother me any further. My partner and I left the house, leaving Evan and Mrs. James on the couch. Mr. James was outside smoking a cigarette. I nodded to him as we got into the car. My partner and I drove off down the bumpy road until we reached the highway. Not a word was uttered.

When I found a safe spot to pull over on the shoulder of the road, I got out of the car, walked to the back of the vehicle, found some grass, and just lost it. I threw up and began sobbing. I cried so hard I lost my breath and began to hyperventilate. My partner placed me in the passenger side of the car and drove us back to our office. By the time we had reached our destination, I had composed myself. I was able to clean up and gather my file on Evan so I could go talk to the judge about what I had just heard and seen.

I walked into the courtroom, and the judge was on the bench, taking pleas. He saw my red, tear-stained face and sensed he needed to call a recess in the morning proceedings. We adjourned to his chambers, and he listened with intent to my morning with the James family. I respected this judge, and he respected me. He was an empathetic and sympathetic man. Evan would be in my office the following Monday, so Judge and I had time to work on a game plan. First, we would order a psychological evaluation on Evan, get his family some help, counseling, find affordable housing, food, clothes, help Mr. and Mrs. James with work, transportation, etc., and get Evan back into school. So many things to do before Monday.

That day was one of the worst of my career as a PO, and, oddly, one of the best. I now knew that Evan did care, but he just didn't know how to ask for help or who to ask it from. Evan and I parted ways as his probation was terminated early due to the circumstances. He and his family did get the help they so desperately needed, thanks to the sympathetic judge who cared and listened.

POODLE PALACE

STEPHANIE — 26
Charged with felony possession of methamphetamine (meth),
1.399 grams
Third offense. Given 10-years probation
Two prior unsuccessful probation terms for possession of
methamphetamine

I served as an adult probation officer in Bexar County for 11 years, and if you were to ask me to rate my absolute *worst* defendant I ever supervised, I would rate Stephanie as the ultimate winner! Stephanie was a sociopath, narcissistic, manipulative, conniving, evil human being, and to make matters worse, she was a mother. The mother of a beautiful 4-year-old red-headed, blue-eyed, precious little girl who would fall victim to her mother's web of lies, deceit, and selfishness.

Stephanie was unsuccessful as a defendant on regular probation. She wasn't in compliance, she lied to her PO, and refused to attend drug/alcohol treatment. Ultimately, she was transferred to my ISP caseload, which meant that Stephanie would remain on probation, but her court-ordered conditions would be stricter. In lieu of reporting to probation only once a month, she would now need to report five times a week, submit to drug tests each weekday, attend drug/alcohol courses plus perform community service hours while maintaining full-time employment.

The judge ordered me to visit her place of employment immediately, so off Mrs. Cullum, my supervisor, and I went. GPS and cell phones had not been invented at this time. It's hard to believe this era even existed, but we headed out with our trusted walkie-talkie and a Mapsco, a city atlas if you will, to locate the address of Stephanie's business. She stated she had owned and operated a pet grooming establishment, known as *THE POODLE PALACE* (would have been an awesome name for a strip club).

After driving for hours, we were unable to find a building with that name because the address Stephanie had given me was a vacant lot. Yes, a vacant lot. Why had Stephanie lied to me? She was in trouble with the court for lying to her previous PO, but now she's lying to me. My job was to file a Motion to Revoke her probation because condition number one: *Do NOT lie to your probation officer about anything.* Including your place of employment.

The next morning, I confronted Stephanie about why she felt compelled to lie, sending my supervisor and me on a wild-goose chase to locate a business that didn't exist. I advised her that a motion to revoke her probation was sitting on the judges' desk, awaiting a hearing date.

Her response, while laughing, was, "Judge won't do anything, he likes me. Oh, and can we hurry up and do my drug test? I have places I have to be."

The drug test, no surprise, was positive for meth, cocaine, and marijuana. This newfound evidence was added to her already prepared pending motion to revoke. Her attorney was notified of his client's pending hearing the next day at 9:00 a.m. sharp, and his presence would be greatly appreciated.

Stephanie had darkened my *office* once, and she had already caused me a great deal of consternation; she had lied to me, tested positive for numerous drugs, and now she's laughing at me. So not cool.

The next morning, I was confident that Stephanie would soon be removed from my caseload due to ongoing noncompliance issues. I sat on the hard wooden pew waiting for the court to begin. Suddenly, the two courtroom doors swung open, and a sudden hush fell into the room as my defendant, Stephanie, and her attorney arrived. Walking in with grand purpose and confidence like a movie star, minus the red carpet, they sauntered in. Stephanie didn't resemble the person I had seen in my office just a day ago. Her blonde hair had been curled with long, wavy locks, her makeup included false eyelashes, and she was wearing a bright pink suit boasting her heaving and voluptuous breasts with a very short skirt. Wearing very high heels, her muscular calves flexed with each stride as she walked to the front pew to take her seat. Every person in that courtroom, including the women, took notice of this creature. Eventually, the judge arrived, and court was underway. We were first on the morning's docket. Judge blushed as Stephanie approached the bench with her attorney.

Judge began to question Stephanie's attorney. "So, Mr. Stanley, why are we here today?"

Hello, ask me, not him, why are we here today, you jackass! His client is continuing to fail her court orders on *intensive supervision probation*, on which YOU, *Your* Honor, placed her. Judge could not keep his eyes off Stephanie's boobs long enough to articulate a logical question as to the lies she presented to me, her officer, and these details had been clearly established in the motion. It was disgusting to watch Judge gush and ogle over Stephanie. Finally, I was able to interject the reason we were all gathered together on this lovely day, but Judge couldn't have been less interested in what I was saying and more interested in her cleavage. Eventually, the violations were heard and placed on record, but without ANY consequences for Stephanie.

I, however, was requested to escort Stephanie, the defendant, to a Narcotics Anonymous (NA) meeting. It is important for you to know that the NA meetings typically took place in the evening after work. Yes, *on my time*, with no overtime or extra compensation. Judge wanted to make sure Stephanie was comfortable with the location *she* had chosen for these NA meetings, and if this location wasn't to her liking, I was to find her a new one. Good grief! I was beginning to feel more like a pimp, rather than a probation officer. I was surprised the judge didn't make me do her laundry, wash her car, and do her grocery shopping.

The next morning, Stephanie arrived for her daily appointment wearing sweatpants and an oversized sweatshirt that read, "LOVE THE ONE YOU'RE WITH," and before she could sit down in the chair, she giggled and, in a snarky tone. "I told you the judge liked me."

Yes, you did.

Skirting the comment, I reminded Stephanie. "Judge has ordered that *we* attend Narcotics Anonymous together, making sure *you* are satisfied with the location and the group that *you* have selected. So, let's plan on meeting tomorrow evening near North Star Mall at 7:00 p.m."

And yes, I was as sarcastic as it sounds.

She agreed, we completed her drug test, and she was on her merry way. The next day after work, I arrived early and waited outside the church where the NA meetings were held. I waited for over an hour, and Stephanie was a no-show. Locating a phone in the church office, I tried calling her home number, but there was no answer.

The next morning, *another* motion to revoke her probation was filed, stating she was a no-show at her NA meeting. As a PO, I was required to file motions whenever a defendant failed to comply with a court-imposed condition of probation. This would be followed by a court hearing before the judge, who had numerous options, including adding more treatment programs or ultimately revoking the defendant's probation and placing them in prison. Intensive Supervision Probation was the last chance before prison, and Stephanie knew this, yet she continued day after day, not doing what she was supposed to.

The following morning, at our next scheduled meeting, I asked Stephanie why she had been a no-show at the meeting.

"I didn't wish to attend a NA meeting, so I went shopping with my daughter and my mom instead. Is that a problem?" she told me as she twirled her blonde hair through her fingers and smacked her gum.

I very patiently reminded her how important these meetings are. "They are designed to give you the tools to help you through your probation and hopefully help you to stop abusing drugs."

She simply stared straight through me without reaction. Stephanie and her attorney reported to court a week later for yet another motion to revoke hearing. Judge was made aware of the most recent issue, same song, second verse, guess what, no consequences from the judge. Just keep reporting daily and continue drug testing.

I won't bore you with the day-to-day activities surrounding

Stephanie's lack of commitment to do anything mandated by the felony judge, but you can well imagine how frustrated I was. This charade continued well into its sixth month. I continued to see and drug test Stephanie daily, and her tests continued to come back positive. Stephanie did not participate in any of her treatment programs, nor was she employed. I lost count after taking Stephanie to court twenty-four times for motions to revoke her probation. So, one day, I just stopped filing these motions. Oh, I continued seeing Stephanie, daily drug tests were performed, but I knew Judge wasn't going to do anything, so why was I wasting my time?

My supervisor became aware of this when an audit of my caseload reflected that I had failed to file motions on Stephanie. I received written and verbal reprimands for not doing my job. This reprimand would be placed in my permanent employee folder, and a very uncomfortable meeting with the Chief ensued.

At our meeting, I sat on 'the couch,' as he stated in a stern voice, "I am very disappointed in you for failing to perform the tasks required of an adult probation officer."

"Yes, Chief, it won't happen again."

My supervisor, Mrs. Cullum, knew the judge wasn't holding Stephanie accountable, but that didn't give me a reason not to perform my job as a PO. Why did I let this defendant and this judge get to me? That "why" would never be answered, so I reinflated my probation officer balloon and got back to work. I began filing motions to revoke on Stephanie's behalf. After all, this defendant and Judge was NOT going to get the better of me. I had a job to do, and do it I would.

Weeks passed, and the last motion I would file to revoke Stephanie's probation had a nail in her preverbal coffin, or so I thought. The facts are as follows:

One very cold and dreary winter evening, around 9:00 p.m., Stephanie went into a bar and began drinking. If this wasn't bad enough, she had taken her little girl with her, leaving her locked in the car for over 4 hours while Stephanie proceeded to party the night away. A patron walking into the bar, passed by the car, saw the little girl in the back seat snuggled under a thin blanket, and called 911.

EMTs arrived, having to break the back window to attend to the child. Stephanie's daughter was diagnosed with hyperthermia, dehydration, malnutrition, and had a fever of one hundred and four. Unaware of the activities surrounding her child, Stephanie was ordering her umpteenth drink and was three sheets to the wind as her daughter was rushed by an ambulance to the nearest hospital.

The little girl was entered into the hospital system as Jane Doe. I was made aware of these events the following morning by Stephanie's mother, who had called to inform me that her daughter and granddaughter hadn't come home the previous evening and to ask whether Stephanie had reported for her regularly scheduled appointment. I told her that I had not seen her yet. Her mother reported that the San Antonio Police arrived at her front door early that morning, explaining they had found Stephanie's ID and that the car located in front of the bar was registered to Stephanie's mom. Stephanie and her daughter lived with her for over a year after Stephanie left her boyfriend.

The mom was beside herself. She was on her way to the hospital to check on her granddaughter, but still had no idea where Stephanie was. The bar closed without any sign of Stephanie, and the bartender witnessed her stumbling out around 2:15 a.m. with an unidentified male. The bar's cameras were not working, leaving the police baffled about Stephanie's whereabouts or who she was with.

After work, I stopped by the hospital to check on the little girl. I quietly entered the hospital room and saw the grandmother sleeping in the chair next to the child's bed, holding a stuffed giraffe in her arms. Hospital equipment beeped while the little girl slept peacefully. The view outside her hospital window presented a beautiful sunset, reminding me that there was still some good on this earth. I exited the room as quietly as I had entered, leaving the grandmother and granddaughter in their hopefully sweet dreams, and I went home.

A hot cup of coffee helped me jump-start the next day, as it was going to be a busy one. I called the detective assigned to Stephanie's case. He reported that there was no sign of her or the gentleman she had left the bar with the previous evening. Three days passed until I received a call from the detective. Stephanie had been picked up wandering the streets, not knowing where she was. She was taken to the emergency room at the same hospital where her daughter was. Stephanie was dehydrated and strung out on drugs. I arrived at the ER in hopes of interviewing her to see if she remembered the events of the evening in question, but she was in no shape to answer any questions. She was handcuffed to the bed since an active warrant had been issued for her, so I figured she would be going nowhere soon.

The next day, I filed my last motion to revoke against Stephanie, alleging her drug and alcohol use and child endangerment of her daughter. The hearing date was to be determined since Stephanie was still hospitalized. Two months passed when the court notified me that the revocation hearing would take place on the upcoming Friday.

On the morning of Stephanie's hearing, I entered a packed courtroom. One of the local TV news crews had cameras set up in the back of the courtroom, and extra bailiffs were assigned that day to contain the crowd. The local news was actually there to tape a highly publicized death sentence that was being announced for a capital murder case; they weren't there for my case.

Stephanie arrived in her finery, displaying the same nonchalant attitude she had carried on throughout her time with me. Her attorney approached me before court, asking what my recommendation would be.

"Revocation and prison time, with intensive drug treatment while she was incarcerated," I told him.

He shook his head in agreement and walked away. Our case would be heard after the capital murder case, and before the court would take a recess for lunch. After the defendant had been given his death date, the judge took a short recess in his chambers, and the news crew was about to begin shutting everything down when I heard one of the news reporters speaking to the cameraman. His eyes were fixated on the beautiful young girl.

"I wonder why she's here, what possible crime could she commit?" he said, smirking to his colleague. "Let's see what this little miss did."

Ten minutes passed when the court bailiff announced, "All rise, the honorable Judge presiding." The judge called our case, and as we approached the bench, I heard Stephanie laughing and, under her breath, saying to her attorney, "Here we go again."

The judge addressed me. "Ms. Moody, for the record, we are here for a revocation hearing citing numerous violations for the defendant, Stephanie James, case number blah, blah, blah...etc, etc., etc., pate bare, step ball change!

"Yes, sir, those are the violations," I responded.

The judge looked up to see the news cameras still in the courtroom, and still filming, so you can imagine his demeanor was very different than the previous twenty-nine times I had brought this defendant before the honorable *CAN'T STOP LOOKING AT HER BOOBS DUDE.*

While standing on the bench, I saw out of the corner of my eye my boss, THE CHIEF, enter the courtroom along with my supervisor. Was I nervous? Yes, but I was prepared for whatever Judge was going to throw my way. The judge asked me what I wished to do with the defendant, and I felt a speech was in order.

"Your honor, may I address the court?"

Judge repositioned himself in his chair, cleared his throat, and responded nervously. "Go ahead, Ms. Moody."

"Your honor, I wish to inform the court that *I am* the individual responsible here, and I have failed to provide the needed services for Ms. James. You see, your honor, the defendant, Ms. James, may be the one who *didn't* perform community service, *didn't* attend her court-ordered drug treatments or NA meetings, while she continued to lie to me daily. Ms. James also tested positive for EVERY SINGLE DRUG TEST while under my supervision. For the record, all of these violations, your honor, were brought to the court's attention twenty-eight times before in previous motions to revoke hearings. Your Honor, in addition to these violations, I would like to advise the court of the defendant's newest violations, as cited in today's motion for revocation. Two months ago, Ms. James made the error of going to a bar and consuming alcohol as well as illegal drugs on the night in question. In addition, the defendant took her 4-year-old daughter to the bar, leaving her in the cold car for over 4 hours with only the warmth of a thin blanket to protect her from the elements, thus resulting in physical and psychological damage to the child."

The audience in the courtroom let out a loud gasp.

"If it hadn't been for a good Samaritan who happened to notice the child in the car," I continued, "I'm not sure her daughter would have survived the 23-degree freezing weather that early morning. The little girl was in the hospital for over a week and lost two toes to hyperthermia. And, Your Honor, I am sure that little girl doesn't understand why someone she trusted left her alone for so long."

At this point, you could hear a pen drop in the courtroom.

"The little girl is safe now and lives with her grandmother. Ms. James is no longer allowed to live in the home and is under strict supervision from child protective services when she visits her daughter. How did I fail Ms. James? Why wasn't Ms. James able to trust me to be there for her, to ask for help? Your honor, considering these circumstances, I have no other choice but to recommend revocation of her probation and request prison time with an intensive inpatient drug/alcohol treatment program while she is in prison to help her with her drug addiction."

The judge was in a trance, gained his composure, and asked, "Is there anything else from Ms. James or her attorney?"

They both shake their heads no.

The Judge continued, "I'm ready to proceed with the revocation of Ms. James probation and sentence her to 5 years in the Texas Department of Criminal Justice. Ms. James, please take advantage of the inpatient drug/alcohol treatment offered in prison. Bailiff, please take Ms. James into custody."

The bailiff handcuffed Stephanie, who was sobbing uncontrollably, and escorted her into the holding cell.

Judge stood and said, "Court is in recess. Ms. Moody, my chambers, NOW!"

I grabbed my paperwork and followed the judge, who was sprinting out of the courtroom into the narrow hall and into his office. Ripping his black robe off and tossing it onto a chair, he slams the chamber door behind me. I could see the veins in his neck as well as the vein that was above the bridge of his nose in the center of his forehead. Both veins looked as if they were about to explode.

He proceeded to scream at the top of his lungs, "HOW DARE YOU MOCK ME IN MY COURTROOM, AND IN FRONT OF TV CREWS!"

A knock at his door by his court coordinator gave a much-needed pause before his rant continued. "NOT NOW!!!!!" he hollered.

A timid voice from the other side of the large door said, "Judge, channel 4 wants to interview you. What do you want me to tell them?"

The judge dashed over to open the door to yell at his sweet, loyal coordinator, but when he did, the camera crew was filming. Judge mustered up a smile, and with a nervous laugh, he said, "Not now, fellas, could we do this a little later?"

The TV anchorwoman and her film crew retreated, assuring the judge they would return later with questions. I walked over to an overstuffed high-back leather chair, kicked my high heels off, and sat down.

"Your honor, I'm sorry if you felt *threatened* out there, but I was doing my job. I wanted everyone in that courtroom to know the details of this endangerment-to-a-child offense. I wanted everyone to know that I had *this* defendant in *your* court twenty-eight times before, and respectfully, if *you* had done *your* job, this may never have happened. What would you have done if that little girl had frozen to death that night?"

I stood up and grabbed my shoes, "Oh, that's right, NOTHING, because you would have blamed it on *me*, the probation officer. Pass the buck as always… so at least I got it on record of what really happened. I also have a written reprimand in my employee file because of this case. I almost got fired because I wasn't doing my job because YOU weren't doing YOURS!"

Barefooted, I walked towards the closed door and opened it to leave. I turned to the judge to add my last two cents. "By the way, had I known there would be a TV film crew in the courtroom today, I would have worn my black dress, NOT this one!"

"BUT WHAT ABOUT MY DOG?"

The court was in recess for lunch, and while I was gathering my things to meet some of the bitches for lunch, the court bailiff approached me to ask if I could counsel an upset defendant. This young man, in his late 20s, had just been sentenced to 6 years in the Texas Department of Corrections for the distribution of heroin. I told the bailiff that I felt uncomfortable because I didn't know what state of emotion the defendant would be in. The bailiff, Joe, assured me that he would call in reinforcements, other bailiffs, while I spoke to the defendant.

With hesitation, I agreed, as the three bailiffs, along with Joe, escorted Gabe, fully shackled from his feet to his hands, from the holding cell. As Gabe exited from the large steel door, I noticed a different man from the one who had just been sentenced. No longer in his starched shirt and dress pants, he was now in bright, obnoxious orange scrubs with BCJ emblazoned on his back while donning the ever-popular slip-on shoes with white socks. His face was red and puffy, and his eyes were bloodshot from crying—and crying hard. The three bailiffs seated the defendant in a chair, flanking him as I sat across the table from them.

"Joe said you wanted to see me? This is very unusual, speaking to a defendant after sentencing, what do you need to speak to me about?" I asked him.

Gabe choked back tears and said, "What about my dog? What's going to happen to my dog?"

My heart sank. "Gabe, you knew that you were going to be sentenced to prison today. Why didn't you take care of this?" I inquired.

"I was hoping for a miracle."

I looked at the bailiff with a question mark on my face, and Joe came to the rescue.

"Ms. Moody can call your landlord. Let's get them on the phone," he told Gabe.

Gabe then contacted his landlord, and arrangements were made for me to go to his apartment after work to pick up his dog. I arrived around 5:30 at Gabe's apartment to be greeted by Jerry, a seventy-five-pound mutt resembling a German Shepherd with curly hair. Jerry was 2-years-old and so excited to see me. He leapt across the room, almost knocking my 5'4" body to the floor. He placed his large paws on my shoulders, as I looked into two big brown eyes. Jerry began licking my face, and I was immediately in love.

I took my newfound furry companion to a friend from my church who had recently lost his dog of 14 years. We spoke from the courthouse, so Gabe was able to speak to Jerry's new owner. The apartment I lived in didn't allow animals, so I wasn't able to take the dog; otherwise, I would have. Since I knew Jerry's new owner, I was able to stay in contact with Jerry, and I even got to dog-sit while his new owners went on vacation.

While Gabe was in prison, I sent him photos of Jerry. They had him posing in front of his new family's Christmas tree, boasting rabbit ears at Easter, and playing in the fall leaves. Gabe was very appreciative that we took the time to save Jerry.

Jerry's new owners changed his name to Riley. He lived on a fifty-acre farm with other animals, had a goose down feather bed near the fireplace, and slept on the down comforter at the feet of his new owner's bed. He also had a large pond at his access for those hot Texas summer days. Jerry lived to be 15-years-old. He was loved beyond measure by his new family, just as Gabe had loved him.

A FETISH IS A FETISH

Taking a report from a registered sex offender had its own challenges, you can be sure of that. On this occasion, Diane was drafting a pre-sentence interview (PSI) for a sex offender. She was writing down information about the defendant, as was the daily common protocol (computers were not used as much as they are today). While writing, her long hair fell into her eyes, and out of habit, she tucked her hair behind her ear, blowing her bangs with a soft whiff of air. The defendant began to breathe heavily and, in a low, growling tone, said, "M-m-m-m-m-m, do that again."

Diane quickly untucked her hair and finished the report. She asked that the defendant please refrain from reacting in that manner again. Diane placed a sticky note in the file, warning individuals who would be in contact with this defendant of the most recent actions. *BEWARE, THIS DEFENDANT EITHER HAS AN EAR OR HAIR FETISH.*

Fetishes are real; we all have them. However, they become a problem in the criminal justice world when a defendant acts inappropriately on these fetishes, possibly leading to some unsavory and criminal activities. Training at the department taught officers and support staff about fetishes and how to prepare should we encounter a defendant with this deviancy. We were taught, first and foremost, that professional attire could prevent arousal in certain defendants. Wearing closed-toe shoes in the office as well as in the courtroom could thwart any actions that might occur should someone have a foot fetish.

Women were also advised to keep the *ta-ta's* and cleavage in control, and proper undergarments, bras, slips, etc., as well as pantyhose were to be worn at all times while in the workplace or in the courtroom.

For men, dress slacks, pressed and creased, with pressed dress shirts tucked and belted, was the appropriate attire. Ties were to be a part of the daily dress code, and socks must be worn with shined shoes. Shorts and tennis shoes were strictly forbidden.

LET SLEEPING JUDGES LIE

Diane was assigned to a misdemeanor court before she began drafting pre-sentence reports for the felony courts. Diane adored her misdemeanor judge, who was in his twilight years. The grandfatherly type, he was one of the sweetest men you would ever want to meet.

I was visiting Diane's court one day when my Judge was in recess, and the court was holding a DWI hearing. We were seated on the side of the bench whispering about where we were going to go to lunch, while a defense attorney was presenting an argument, when I unexpectedly heard the judge snoring ever so quietly. No one in the courtroom noticed except Diane and me. Trying to keep this our secret, Diane, donning her dress and heels, crawled up the three steps next to Judge. Completely unnoticed, she began tugging ever so lightly at the hem of the judge's robe, "Pppsssstttt... Judge, Judge?"

He quietly snorted and woke up, pivoting his chair around to see Diane crouched on the floor. He turned his chair back to the task at hand, not before winking a much appreciative thank you towards Diane. The court continued without incident.

Going above and beyond the call of duty is just one of the many services offered by a devoted officer protecting her judge's reputation.

MURDER HE WROTE

I made a rule for myself not to open a new defendant's file until I met the individual. I wanted to hear the facts of the case straight from the horse's mouth, so to speak, before any 'judgements' were passed.

Tall, dark, and handsome walked into my office for his first appointment, wearing an expensive suit, a navy and red striped tie, donning leather penny loafers attached to bright red and gray argyle socks. Very preppy. Recognizing the man who stood in my *shower/office*, I took an inaudible gasp. I recognized him from the recent evening, six o'clock, and ten o'clock news. Snippets from his trial had recently been broadcast, showing the defendant seated in the courtroom next to his defense attorney, crying and visibly emotional. The 12-person jury had made a unanimous decision to place this newly convicted felon on 10 years of probation for manslaughter.

Preppy Pete had a smile and charisma oozing from his pores. He looked as if he had just walked off the pages of a GQ magazine ad for clothes, boxers or briefs, cologne, toothpaste, you name it, he could've sold it.

He extended his hand, shook mine with a gentle but firm grip, and smiled, showing off his pearly whites. His voice was low and melodious as I instructed him to take a seat. I introduced myself, explaining a few ISPs, a.k.a. probation housekeeping rules and guidelines that the court had placed upon him. He was advised he would have to report to me in person twice a week until further notice. He gently nodded in agreement while I had his still-closed case file on my desk, asking him to please share the details that led to his involvement with the judicial system.

He cleared his throat, giggled ever so lightly, and stated, "Well, I just got away with murder."

"Excuse me?" I remarked.

Continuing to smile, he repeated, "I killed one of my six-month-old twin boys."

"I saw you on television. You were upset, crying uncontrollably."

"An Oscar-winning performance, wouldn't you say?" he casually responded.

I remember feeling nauseous and angry while trying to maintain some modicum of professionalism. I was dealing with a psychopath, and I knew this case would test me to my core. His story is as follows:

"My wife and I were excited to start a family. We had been married for 3 years, and I am a managing partner for a marketing firm; my work takes me all over the world. Our first few years of marriage were like a 3-year honeymoon, traveling and enjoying life, but then Amy became pregnant. We decided to settle here in San Antonio because Amy is from here, and her parents and grandparents all live here. Amy has a twin sister, and their family resides about an hour from San Antonio. I'm an only child, lost my parents tragically when I was a teenager. My grandparents, who lived in another state, were my only family, and they are gone now, so it's just me, an island. I remember the day of the sonogram when we discovered that twins were on the way. Amy was so happy. It was difficult for me to show excitement over the news, but I powered through it for Amy. I wanted to have a child. *A child*, not two. Two children were not in my life plan."

I interrupted him for a moment to remind him of his current surroundings, asking sarcastically, "How did this plan work out for you?"

Not proud of myself for leaving the professional realm for that moment, but I did, and I said it.

Glaring at me with his navy-blue eyes, he continued, "We moved into our dream home, and we knew we were having twin boys, so blue was everywhere in the nursery. Amy was glowing with excitement. Her ob-gyn placed her on bed rest for the last six weeks of the pregnancy, so I hired a full-time nurse to be with her, helping her out when I was out of town. I didn't travel for the last two weeks of the pregnancy, waiting for the twins' arrival. I look back on those last few weeks with great fondness, because it was just Amy and me. We watched movies, I cooked, and I knew it would never be the same again once the boys were born. The twins arrived, each weighing about four pounds, so they stayed in the hospital for two weeks to gain weight before they could come home. We were at the hospital morning, noon, and night, only coming home to get a few hours of sleep each night. Everything changed. Amy was a mother now; those two boys were her life, and I was put on the back burner. Oh, I know she loved me, but it was just different. Everyone was gaga over Amy and the twins. I ceased to exist, so I returned to work about a month after Amy and the boys were settled. She had her mom and sister almost living at the house to help. I was never alone with Amy or the boys. I couldn't catch my breath, and I was always in a panic and anxious state. The only place I felt at home was at the office. The day of the event, I was putting one of our sons into the car seat when Edwin would NOT stop crying. I absolutely lost it, and I banged that little guy's head into the back of the car seat repeatedly until he was quiet."

Peter adjusted his suit jacket and tie, wiping the sweat beads from his top lip with his freshly starched handkerchief, which he had taken from his pocket. I excused myself, took my coffee cup, and said I needed more water. Consumed with such anger and sadness, I sprinted to the ladies' room where I threw up in the trash can. Rinsing my mouth out with water and sleeking my hair down, I returned to my office/shower.

Preppy Pete noticed my appearance and asked, "Are you all right? You're really pale; you might be coming down with something."

"No, I'm fine, probably lunch not agreeing with me," I lied.

Trying to continue the interview to the best of my ability, I asked Peter where his wife was. He told me that he and Amy had recently separated, and she and the baby were living with her sister and her family.

"Are ya'll seeing a professional therapist?" I asked.

Excited and enthusiastic, he responded, "No, do you think that would help? The court won't allow me to be alone with my other son.

Can you believe that?"

"Yes, Peter, I can. It's for the safety of your son."

"Can you help me see my son?"

"Not at this time, Peter. When and if that time comes, you will have to be under the supervision of a court liaison."

"You mean someone will have to watch me when I am with my *own* flesh and blood?"

"Yes, it's in everyone's best interest, but let's take this a week at a time, shall we? You have programs to attend, community service to complete, and work to do. Focus on that for the time being." I scheduled our next appointment and realized I was dealing with my first psychopath. Let the journey begin.

Months passed, and Preppy Pete completed his stress management class and parenting class, and, in lieu of community service, the judge allowed Pete to pay money to his favorite charity. I wished the judge had encouraged Peter to complete his community service in person. I felt he needed to get his hands dirty and do something for the community and himself, but I'm not the judge.

Amy and Pete eventually divorced, and she got a job and moved out of state with their twin son, who was now over 2 years of age. Peter wanted to see his son, but the court repeatedly denied his request. He wasn't allowed to leave Bexar County without permission from the court and had to obtain permission from the judge to leave the state. A year later, the holiday season came, and Peter asked Judge to see his son. He received permission to travel to see his son once Amy approved. The visit would have to be supervised, so arrangements were made. At our appointment, after Peter had visited his ex and his son, he reported that he and Amy were reuniting and he would be relocating to Seattle, Washington. The judge had his probation transferred, and the psychopath would be off my caseload and out of my life. I wonder if Amy was aware of Peter's psychosis and what she would do if she knew what Peter had told me at our very first meeting. I hope their story turned out with a happily ever after instead of a happily never after.

GANGS 101

In 1993, San Antonio's population was 936,000; by 2023, it had risen to 1,479,493. In 1993, there were approximately 1,260 gang-related drive-by shootings called in to the San Antonio Police Department (SAPD) dispatch, and SAPD estimates that for every drive-by that was called in, ten would not be reported. By contrast, just up I-35, about an hour away in Austin, Texas, there were only fifty drive-by shootings that same year. Fun fact, neither Houston, Texas, nor El Paso, Texas kept figures on drive-by shootings, but would classify the shootings as an assault or a homicide, depending on the outcome.

Drive-by shootings are triggered by turf/territory wars, fights with or over a girlfriend, initiations into gangs, throwing hand signs at rival gangs, or just for the hell of it. Guns used in these shootings are purchased at nearby pawn shops and gun shows. An interesting fact: in Texas, you are able to attend multiple gun shows on any given weekend throughout the state, all legal, but to purchase a weapon, an individual must be at least 21. Other guns that are used for the purpose of drive-by shootings may be purchased illegally on the street, or guns that have been stolen are used in these shootings.

Joining a gang has numerous forms of initiation. These range from 'jumpin-in' to severe beatings from current gang members, or new recruits may have to perform acts of rape, shoplifting, robbery, burglary, stealing a gun, assaulting a rival gang member, drive-by shootings, or self- mutilation.

There is a ranking system used in the gangs. The boss is the leader, while the underboss is second in command. The captain is responsible for field activities and recruiting new members. Soldiers or gangsters are the typical gang members who commit the gang's activities. Associates, or hang-arounds, are people who are not full members of the gang but who support or participate in gang activities.

Should a member of a gang wish to quit and relinquish their membership, the gang members will perform similar initiations by beating the newly outed member so severely that serious injury or death may be the result.

According to SAPD stats, in the early 1990s, San Antonio was home to approximately 2,000 hard-core gang members. Los Angeles had the worst gang problem in the United States at this time, and we were catching up fast. Citizens of San Antonio were frustrated by the number of drive-by shootings and the deaths of innocent people, including babies dying in their cribs at night because of these senseless acts.

A task force made up of judges, lawyers, and law enforcement traveled to Los Angeles to observe firsthand the inner workings of gangs, their activities, legal and otherwise. This task force wanted to get a handle on what we were dealing with to better understand gangs. With this new knowledge, SAPD formed a Gang Unit. The unit has proven effective and remains part of SAPD today. The Gang Unit is a subunit of the Covert Response Unit of the Texas Anti-Gang (TAG) unit.

The new age crimes that are committed by 21st-century gang members are: sex trafficking, racketeering, murder, drug trafficking, weapons smuggling, and human smuggling. And sadly, drive-by shootings still occur today. In the 90s, the *blood-in, blood-out* rule required lifetime membership from a gang member, but the younger members of today aren't as rigorous with this rule as their predecessors.

Every year, adult probation officers are required to complete 40 hours of continuing education in the probation field to keep their certifications/licensures current. GANG TRAINING 101 turned out to be one of my favorite annual courses. Gang bangers would come talk to us, show us their tattoos, the ones they could reveal anyway. A former gang member showed us his tattoo that covered his entire back. This tattoo was a beautiful and colorful Madonna, Jesus' mother, the Virgin Mary, not the singer (this tattoo is referenced in an earlier chapter). He said he got it before he entered the prison system in hopes that it would keep him from getting punk'd or raped in prison. Sadly, this did not deter the inmates from this horrible act of prison initiation.

Notably, in the early 1990s, only gang members had these works of art; today, tattoos are part of our culture, and nearly everyone has one (FYI, I do not have one, nor ever plan on getting one). Former gang bangers, men and women who had aged out of this lifestyle, would also come and educate us about the most recent gang news and share with us recent deaths from drive-bys, drug overdoses, etc. Basically, stuff that didn't reach the news or the newspapers. The kind of stuff that would keep me up at night. I was raised in West Texas, where we didn't have problems like gangs, so I found this world of gangdom to be fascinating.

There are approximately fourteen gangs in San Antonio today. The Latin Kings, Texas Mexican Mafia, Soranos, Texas Syndicate, Aryan Brotherhood of Texas, Aryan Circle, Bandidos, Bloods, Crips, Gangster Disciples, and Peckerwood, just to name a few.

There were numerous boy gangs and girl gangs in San Antonio, and these gangs were organized by race. The largest gang was on the north side of San Anton and was referred to as the Anglos. Hispanic gangs were located on the west side, in the Alazon Apache Court area, while the African American gang members were on the east side. The Hispanic credo was Familia and turf, while the African American gangs were more individualistic. These gangs were involved in business ventures, prostitution, and the sale of crack. Drive-bys are only used by this gang if someone tries to cut into their business; otherwise, they leave you alone.

The ND Chicks were a girl gang located in the Alazon Apache Court area, and it is alleged that they hated the LA Boyz, a local boy gang. The girls did not use weapons, but they loved to fight. It's reported that they learned to fight from the guys because they "took pain from the guys." The girls liked to hit other girls in the face to "mess them up." Girls in gangs were proud to show their bruised and bloody faces as a badge of honor, so to speak. Pushing and kicking to really humiliate another was part of the repertoire, as well as having a rival gang member "kiss the rag" (kiss the green bandanna, the ND

Chicks' colors). Their mascot was Notre Dame's fighting Irishman with hands holding an Uzi.

These girls attended a local middle school, but attending classes was not part of the daily routine. Instead of learning, they preferred to hang out with their "homies" and smoke pot. Gang initiations into girl gangs would involve having sex threesomes, being a part of a sex train, where several guys take turns having sex with one girl while others look on.

The LA Boyz were founded by a group of young men who were football players from Lanier High School. These boys wanted to be a part of something, so a gang was born. They had a lot of parties and always had several girls at these functions. The LA Boyz colors were yellow, and their mascot was a yellow Tweety Bird holding a gun.

YOU NEVER FORGET YOUR FIRST

BEAUX — 28
Charged with delivery of LSD, first-degree felony
Two prior drug offenses; probation satisfactorily served on both
One prior prison term of five years for delivery of drugs,
prison term served
Member of a local gang

Beaux was the first gang member I had ever met, outside of the annual gang training I received. He was also the first gang member that I supervised as a probation officer, and as they always say, you never forget your first.

Beaux was my defendant's gang name; that is how I referred to him when he reported for his appointments, three times a week. He was placed on my caseload because he was not living up to his mandated conditions, and if he did not complete his probation with me, he would be going to prison for 10 years.

When I met Beaux, he was active in a local male gang and was not employed in a legal occupation. He informed me that he would not work in a legal profession, as it was a *joke what they pay*. He wasn't lying, tell me about it, my pay absolutely was a joke!

Beaux lived in Alazon Apache Court, one of San Antonio's roughest housing projects. Everyone in the projects knew him and his posse. Beaux told me he was only 10 when he joined the gang and dropped out of school in the seventh grade. He said he started drinking at the age of six. He was mostly raised by his mom. She worked full-time, while his dad drank all day and beat the living @#$%^&* out of him and his two brothers almost every day. Beaux said his dad never beat his sister or his mother. His dad left them when he was eleven. Beaux said that was the happiest day ever, and he hadn't seen him since. He said he resided with his mom and one brother, who was also in the gang.

"People think we're in gangs because our folks don't love us, but it ain't notin' like that. We join because, you know?" Beaux told me, shrugging his shoulders.

His oldest brother was killed by a rival gang member during a drive-by 5 years ago.

Beaux said, "Mom still ain't over that. Guess I'm not either."

"Have you ever been involved in a drive-by?' I asked him.

"Yeah, you know," he shrugged. "We get pumped up and do a drive by, or you know."

"Your sister? Where is she?" I inquired.

"She dead too, she did it herself."

Beaux appeared nervous and began to clear his throat and fidget in the chair.

"Want to talk about it?" I offered.

"Do I haff tu?" he asked.

"No, but I'm a good listener if you do want to talk about it."

"K," he said.

Beaux reported on time, usually, and he would always request my last appointment of the day. He would sleep all day, party all night, and do 'gang stuff,' so the 'later the better' worked out for his busy schedule. I had been Beaux's probation officer for about two months when he opened up about his sister. It was her birthday, and he was missing her, so on this day, I was to learn the awful truth of his sister's death.

As he began to speak of the details involving her, he started to cry. This big, burly, tattooed, gang-banger started to cry, and cry hard. Handing him a box of tissues, I just let him cry until he couldn't cry anymore. I think he really needed it; you know that deep, cathartic, cleansing cry? The kind of cry that exhausts you and leaves you feeling like you just ran half a marathon. That kind of cry.

Beaux apologized to me for 'letting loose' like that.

"No apologies necessary," I told him.

We sat in complete silence in my office for a period, until he had stopped crying and was breathing slowly and methodically, trying to get the nerve to tell me what had happened on the day of his sister's death. Patiently, I waited for him to begin.

"I begged my little sister not to get involved. Gangs, you know? The day she did it, we had a jumpin' in."

I looked befuddled because Beaux had to explain the process.

"It's where we get newbies joining," he explained, and I nodded.

"We beat the living @#$&^%! out of these guys, blood is flying, it's all over everywhere. Afta, we hug it out." Beaux smiled, then continued. "And then, we get waaaaasssstttted!!!!! I respect yoose Miss, so what I'm about to say, I'm kinda embarrassed, you know?"

"Take your time."

Beaux continued. "We boys do girl nights, too. Alllllllll the lights are out in this bedroom, so dark, you can't see nuttin. A girl wants to join, yoose know, a gang, so she's blindfolded, and well, we all will pull a train. She don't know who is duin what til afta, then the girl is n' this circle. We all there, round hur, still wear'n the fold, and she takes it off."

Beaux started sobbing again. "The girl, in the circle, she my sista."

My heart and stomach fell to the bottom of my feet. I didn't respond. I felt like screaming, but sat still in my chair.

"Sis sees me, I sees her, she run out, her homies go wit. My boys look at me, and they are like, you know, WHAT@#^$&%*^(&)()#_? They said they din't know she was wuntin in, they swore. They wuldn't have #$%&)#() my sis knowin' it was hur," Beaux said, pausing. "She wuz miss'n fur days, police come to mom's, told her, sis had hung herself. I nev'a told my mom whut really hapn'd,"

As you can imagine, Beaux was still emotional. I had joined the cry choir as well. Call it unprofessional, but I couldn't help myself.

I wept for this young man, for this brother, for this son who couldn't disclose to his mom the actual events that led up to her own daughter's death. What a burden Beaux would have to carry for the rest of his life. I contacted the psychologist; she took him to her office for further counseling. Beaux continued to report three times a week for many more months. We never spoke about his sister or what had happened to her.

To no one's surprise, Beaux was not successful on probation and would end up serving a 10-year term for new delivery of drugs charges.

SO... THIS PRIEST WALKS IN...

FATHER DONAGHY – 58
Charged with aggravated assault, second-degree felony
No priors, Given 5-years probation
(He was a priest in full priestly regalia, black pants, black shirt,
black socks, black shoes, white color, a bible, you get the picture)

In my second year as an officer in the Intensive Supervision Probation (ISP) Unit, I met my first priest, a man of the cloth, a Catholic priest. A Priest, on felony probation? His name was Father Patrick Donaghy, a good Irish Catholic. *Or was he?* When he spoke, he had a slight Irish brogue, which at first, I found to be charming, but let me tell you that charm would wear off quickly.

When I met Father D., he had already been on probation for over a year, and I can honestly say, out of all the years and all the hundreds of people I would encounter as a PO, Father D. was the MOST DIFFICULT defendant I ever supervised. When he reported for his appointments, I would have to do the hokey-pokey and talk myself into a positive, happy place before calling him up. He was rude, arrogant, obstinate, and he hated women in authority, but most of all, he was unwilling to take responsibility for his crime.

Father D. was placed in ISP due to a contempt of court charge. He argued and pissed the judge off by refusing to take his Anger Management course and to complete 200 hours of community service.

"My job *is* community service. I shouldn't have to perform any hours!" The priest argued.

The judge disagreed and placed him under my watch. Instead of reporting monthly, Father D. would now have to report twice a week and was threatened that he needed to complete the course and hours ASAP, or else.

It took numerous meetings, but Father D. finally started working on his hours. I had him perform his community service at the San Antonio Food Bank, place flags on veterans' graves at the military cemetery, and walk dogs at the animal shelter. The Anger Management course would take longer to get him to start that eight-week journey, but baby steps.

The facts of Father D's case are as follows: One sunny spring Saturday, Father D. took his parishioners to a Planned Parenthood location where they would protest abortions. Placards with colored photos of dead fetuses were being hoisted by parishioners as traffic whizzed by, hoping to make a point to the onlookers. This is where it gets icky. An innocent woman, 29 years of age, attempts to enter the Planned Parenthood facility when Father D. steps over the designated protest line, lunging at this poor woman. He proceeds to take his placard and begins to stab her with the wooden stake attached to the placard. An employee from inside comes to her aid, pulling Father D. off her. Paramedics and police arrived soon, arresting Father D. and rushing this woman to the nearest hospital, where she underwent 6 hours of surgery.

The victim's recovery lasted many months. She was rendered blind in one eye, suffered a broken leg on one leg, a broken ankle on the other, a broken back, and bruising all over her face and body. One of the male parishioners described the beating as he watched:

"It was happening in slow motion. You saw what was happening, but you couldn't believe what you were seeing."

The Catholic diocese ended up being responsible for paying for the woman's surgery, psychiatric care, and follow-up surgeries. Father D. was relocated to a new parish where he continued to perform his daily Mass schedule and his Saturday evening Masses.

One day, I had a scheduled appointment with Father D., and I was running fifteen minutes behind. Father D. would breach through security and was standing in my doorway, berating me, screaming at the top of his lungs, causing quite a scene. Security escorted the priest out of the building, instructing him to leave and cool off, and that I would notify him of a new appointment. The next morning, at our new meeting time, I asked why he was so agitated with me.

"None of your business!" he shouted.

"Sir, you disrupted the entire waiting room, upset the probationer I was meeting with when you came into my office, so yes, it is my business."

Father D. replied loudly. "I don't belong here, and I CERTAINLY DO NOT NEED TO BE SITTING DOWN THERE WAITING FOR YOU WITH ALL THOSE CRIMINALS!"

I opened his file to the colored photos of the victim, turning the folder so that he could view the bruised and beaten body of the woman he so senselessly attacked.

Looking over his shoulder, he shrugged, looked me square in the face with his dark and dead eyes, and said, "She deserved every bit of what I did to her, and more."

I could feel my blood pressure rise and my face becoming hot and red. "Sir?"

"You heard me!" he said. "I didn't do anything wrong."

My retort. "Thou shalt not kill, does that ring a bell?"

He smirked, leaned toward the desk, and smugly whispered, "She didn't die, did she?"

I remember having to take a deep, cleansing breath before speaking.

"No, Sir, but she almost did. Father D., let me ask this: of all the women who entered the facility that morning, why did you choose to attack her?"

"She was going in for an abortion."

"How did you know that?" I asked.

His reply was, "That's what women do."

I advised Father D. that Planned Parenthood offered numerous services other than abortion procedures. Education, birth control, and vasectomies.

"Would you have attacked a man who was going in for a vasectomy?"

No response. He just kept glaring me down with those soulless eyes.

"Father D., the woman that you attacked at the facility," I told him as he still glared at me. "She was a nun."

His face grew ashen and pale.

"The Sister has been going to Planned Parenthood for years. She counsels young women and encourages them to place their unborn babies up for adoption. She connects these women with doctors and lawyers to help navigate their pregnancy so they can give up their child to loving families," I informed him.

He was still speechless. I slid an appointment card across my desk showing Father D. our next meeting time.

After Father D. completed his community service hours and the Anger Management course, I returned him to regular monthly reporting and back to his original officer to complete his three remaining years of probation. I would see him occasionally in the waiting room, and he was still rude, arrogant, and demanding his importance.

"Judge not, lest ye be judged." Matthew 7.

I heard the nun had to have additional surgeries, but once she was strong enough, she continued her counseling at Planned Parenthood. I admire her commitment and her resilience. The world needs more people like her.

WRONG PLACE AT THE RIGHT TIME

As an adult probation officer, I was required to conduct home visits to defendants assigned to my caseload. This offered up the opportunity for us to see firsthand how our defendants lived, or didn't live. Probation officers were not allowed to go to a defendant's home without a walkie-talkie (pre-cell phone days), and *never, ever,* should go alone. Always take a buddy, preferably someone you like.

In the early 90s, probation officers were not allowed to carry weapons; however, I would carry pepper spray. Before leaving the office, we had to sign a home visit log that recorded the defendant's name, case number, and the address where the home visit would take place. These visits were done randomly. Sometimes defendants would be home, and sometimes at work. We never interrupted a defendant at their place of employment; we didn't want to embarrass them if their boss wasn't aware they were on probation.

On a very hot Texas summer day, around three in the afternoon, and 103-plus degrees outside, Ann and I headed out to visit one of my defendants, Luis, who was placed on a five-year probation term for felony third-degree possession of cocaine.

Arriving at Luis' home, Ann went through the side chain-link fence, positioning herself at the back door. I approached the front door, no doorbell, knocking, and simultaneously announcing myself. "Luis, this is Ms. Moody from probation."

From inside, I immediately heard furniture being shoved around and footsteps running across the hardwood floors.

"I'll be right there, just give me a sec."

"Luis, are you ok?" I asked.

"Yeah, just hang on."

As I detected panic in his voice, I grew nervous. Luis placed the security chain on the door, opening wide enough for me to see half of my defendant's sweaty head. To the right side of his face, I saw a round wooden coffee table. Perched in the middle of this table, a very large mound of white, powdery substance, a scale, baggies, and steel implements were shining like a brightly lit beacon in the sun's reflection, when I noticed the handle of a Glock under the scale.

Ignoring what I had seen, or at least not letting Luis know, I asked, "Luis, how are you? Just checking in to see how you're doing?"

"Fine, fine, Ms. Moody, what's up?"

"Home visit time, Luis," I told him as I hit the silent panic button on the walkie-talkie, advising my partner Ann that I needed assistance.

My instinct told me to get the hell out of there and FAST! Acting as if I had received a call on the walkie-talkie, I handed Luis my business card. "Luis, I have to get back to the office. Will you call for your next appointment?" I asked."Yes, ma'am, sure will," he said as he slammed the door.

I leisurely began walking down the sidewalk towards the car. Thankfully, Ann heard the conversation from the back door of the house and had alerted our office and the San Antonio Police. Safely inside the car with the ignition running, we heard the police vehicles approaching as we exited the street. As it turns out, the police arrested Luis for possession of cocaine, paraphernalia, and firearms. Two men were found hiding in the back bedroom in a closet with loaded weapons, and these two men were also taken into custody.

While searching the house, the police found a book under the coffee table, which listed the names and phone numbers of people of interest, and they were very excited about it. The feds got involved, and in the end, a lot of very bad people were going to be spending many years under the love and care of the federal penitentiary system. I know that day could have turned out totally different; our lives could have changed in the blink of an eye. Wrong place, right time, but all in all, a good day.

TEN THOUSAND CLAMS

JORGE — 29
Charged with felony delivery of cocaine
No priors. Given 10-years probation

Typically, delivery of cocaine charges in large amounts would be tried in the federal courts; however, the feds didn't want Jorge's case, so it was passed to the state prosecutors to handle. A jury trial allowed Jorge to be given probation. He probably should have been in the state pen, but instead, a jury of his peers granted him probation.

I will put this as delicately as I can. Jorge was an asshole, a complete and utter *asshole*! He was so disruptive on the day of his sentencing that the judge held him in contempt for disrespecting the court. Jorge was placed immediately into Intensive Supervision Probation, which required Jorge to report on Mondays, Wednesdays, and Fridays in lieu of monthly appointments.

Drug tests would have to be performed at each of these appointments, and on the day of the sentencing, the judge had Jorge perform a drug test to get a baseline of the drugs that were in the defendant's system. As you can imagine, Jorge tested positive for meth, cocaine, and marijuana. The numbers were off the charts. The judge warned Jorge that if he did not see the drug numbers decline, he would place him in prison without any hesitation.

Yay me. I was the chosen one assigned to this douche bag. Our first meeting was tough. Jorge was rude, argumentative, and, surprise, surprise, his drug test was off the charts for all the aforementioned chemicals. Per the court's instructions, the judge was notified of the positive tests and instructed that, due to the upcoming Christmas holidays, I was to continue drug testing three times a week at our scheduled appointments. Christmas came on a Monday that year, so I couldn't meet with Jorge until Wednesday of that week.

Jorge came in 2 hours late. As he entered my office, he positioned himself in the wooden chair and, from under his heavy winter coat, retrieved a large manila envelope. Jorge ever so gently slid the package across my desk, placing it in front of me. I locked eyes with the defendant, praying it was a late Christmas present, but when I opened the envelope, it revealed a rather large sum of money.

Jorge winked at me and announced, "We ain't doing no drug test today, do we understand each other?"

I knew that Jorge had entered the building through our metal detector, so I hoped he wasn't stupid enough to carry a gun. Or would he? One of my co-workers, seated across from me in the nearest office, saw the look on my face and *Thank God*, she alerted security and my supervisor that something was amiss in River City. As I conducted our tri-weekly interview, not letting Jorge know that my heart was pounding out of my chest, three security men arrived along with my supervisor. The defendant was handcuffed and taken to a holding room, the money from the envelope was placed in a large evidence bag, and I notified the court.

The judge requested that Jorge, I, and the three security officers, along with an armed San Antonio police officer, escort Jorge to court as "quickly as we could get him there."

Arriving within ten minutes, the judge asked for the evidence bag containing the manila envelope. He looked inside, flipped through the money, handed the loot to the court bailiff, and asked that it be counted. *Ten thousand dollars* were in that envelope. Still donning the handcuffs, Jorge was summoned to the bench, cussing and swearing as the bailiffs placed him in front of the Judge.

"Ms. Moody, how did this money come into your possession?"

I explained the recent events to the court, and the judge sentenced Jorge to 25 years for bribing an officer. Jorge demanded that the money be given back to his family, but the judge laughed and said, "No, sir, these funds are now property of Bexar County."

As the bailiffs escorted the defendant out of the courtroom and into the holding facility, Jorge used words that I had never heard. Then he yelled, "If that BITCH (pointing in my direction) had just taken the F@#$*%(^) money, I wouldn't be here!"

BRIBE: Persuade (someone) to act in one's favor, typically, illegally or dishonestly, by a gift of money or other inducement. EXTORTION, BRIBE, PAYOFF, HUSH MONEY.

Hush money, my ass. There is no amount of money that I would have taken. My conscience, and let's not forget to mention my moral compass, wouldn't have allowed it. Good thing Jorge was assigned to my caseload, because I'm not sure another officer in my court wouldn't have taken the money, and that, my dear readers, is another story.

"O BROTHER, WHERE ART THOU?"

ALLEN — 48
Charged with murder, reduced to manslaughter
No priors. Given 6-years probation
Probation granted by a jury after a 2-week trial

Over the years, I met defendants who would push every button I had. They were demanding, obtuse, rude, arrogant, and somehow blamed society for their unfortunate lot in life, but not Allen. Allen had committed the worst crime known to man; he had taken a life.

I had seen the six o'clock news feed showing Allen crying throughout his trial, and not crying because he was innocent, but crying because he knew he was guilty. Guilty of killing not only his best friend, who coincidentally was also his brother, but also taking full responsibility for this horrific action. Without a doubt, Allen was my favorite defendant out of all the hundreds of people I supervised over my 11 years as a PO. He was kind, respectful, humble, patriotic, but mostly remorseful.

Allen was a tall man, standing 6'2". He had a ruddy complexion, dirty blonde hair, a handsome physique, and deep bluish-purple eyes. Allen never married or had children, but he loved his family and his country. He had no interest in college, so he joined the military upon graduating from high school. After serving his country for 10 years, he began working as a truck driver for a local company in San Antonio. Eventually, he purchased his own eighteen-wheeler and became a long-haul truck driver, delivering across the United States and parts of Mexico. He pulled in six figures easily, and in the early 90s, that was a great deal of the green. He was saving his money so he could buy a hunting lodge for himself and his brother. They were planning to relocate to Colorado once he retired. His brother, Steve, was a taxidermist, a true artist, and was well sought after in Texas. After all, we are a state that loves to hunt.

This is Allen's story:

Allen had returned home from a month-long driving gig to the house he shared with his brother Steve. Upon entering his bedroom, Allen was shocked to find his brother, who was his confidant and best friend, in bed with his girlfriend. A physical fight broke out, and the girlfriend grabbed her clothes and fled from the home. Steve and Allen continued fist fighting and ended up in the bathroom. Allen was beyond rage and not thinking as he picked up an umbrella and began to stab his brother numerous times with the sharp end of it.

Allen stated that at the time of the altercation, he wasn't even aware that he stabbed Steve; it was as if he was having an out-of-body experience. At one point, he realized what he had done and called 911. He was taken into custody, and the criminal justice process began.

By the time of my first appointment with Allen, he had attempted suicide and was in counseling. I have never encountered anybody so broken and sad. My heart ached for him and his family. During our first six months together, I had Allen report daily to help him get into a routine, as he had lost his job after being placed on probation. He wasn't allowed to leave the county, so his job as a truck driver was put on hold. Job counseling helped him find work as a busser and barback at a restaurant. Working kept him busy and gave him a sense of purpose.

Community service also provided a positive outlet for Allen. He cleaned tombstones and did gardening at the Veterans Cemetery in San Antonio. Being outdoors, going to counseling, and working helped Allen to regain some of his confidence. Eventually, he completed all his court-mandated programs and community service and paid his fees and court costs. After 2 years, the court allowed Allen to resume driving his truck and delivering only in Texas. His mother and family had been in group counseling together, working on healing and dealing with the consequences of Steve's death. It was a slow process, but love and forgiveness reigned supreme in this case.

Allen had served 4 years of his probation term when I petitioned for him to be terminated early satisfactorily. I felt he had suffered enough and would have to live with his demons for the remainder of his life.

A few years later, I received a letter at my office with photographs attached to it with a paper clip; it was from Allen. The photos revealed a happily married couple standing in front of a beautiful lodge nestled in the green trees kissed with newly fallen snow. The enclosed photographs looked like postcards. Allen and his new bride had purchased a beautiful lodge in Colorado, the one he hoped to share with his brother.

It was an odd irony, but life is funny and weird beyond words. Allen's life and that of his family took a tragic turn, but finding happiness in the bleakness brought courage for him and his new wife. God speed, Allen, God speed.

A BABY... WITH A GUN!

Each defendant or probationer had to pass through a metal detector upon entering our building before registering to see their probation officer. While I was with the Bexar County Probation Department, we didn't have hand-wand detectors, and due to budget constraints, we didn't have an X-ray to view bags, purses, etc. Each bag had to be searched by one of our illustrious security teams, consisting of all men, and they took their job very seriously. The process was archaic and labor-intensive, but it was a measure of security that I was glad we had.

As probation officers, we are trained to observe people, paying attention to their oddities, gestures, the way they walk, and the way they talk. Observing body language is sometimes more telling than the words that come out of a person's mouth. I feel that you are also born with an innate ability to observe. I view this as a plus when you are a PO. I have always been an avid 'voyeur' of the human species; we are fascinating, whether in a group or alone. People watching is a great way to pass the time, especially at airports, train/subway stations, concerts, lectures, plays, and even at the movies.

Next time you are at one of these locations or events, I strongly urge you to put that book down, get off your phone, and just observe and people-watch. I provide this background to help you better understand the next story.

It was a typical hot and sunny summer day, and I was in a hurry to get into the air conditioning as quickly as possible. A friend dropped me off at the front door of our building after we had lunch, and I entered through the same door as every other person, employee, or defendant. Defendants formed lines on the right, and employees swerved left without going through the metal detector. A security officer was assigned to the defendant line, ensuring all defendants followed security protocol before reaching the metal detector.

A woman in her mid-20s was entering the department at the same time that I had arrived. I observed this woman enter the building carrying more than was almost humanly possible. On one arm, she carried a large diaper bag, and her other arm was consumed with a purse. She was trying to push a baby stroller with a very young baby through the front door. Having difficulty getting her baby stroller over the door threshold, I helped her by lifting the front of the stroller, allowing the front wheels to touch the floor with ease. I felt bad for this woman having to lug a baby and all that comes with it, especially on such a hot day. I looked up at her, hoping to see a smile, but noticed the pupils of her eyes. They were largely dilated, dark, and soulless. She was sweating heavily; her frame was small and petite, malnourished, and her skin was pale, almost translucent. She was wearing a short-sleeved T-shirt and Daisy Dukes (sadly, those have come back into fashion). I didn't notice any needle tracts on either of her arms or her legs, and there were no visible scars, sores, or bruising. She was clearly nervous, looking over each shoulder as she waited for her turn to enter the metal detector.

I suppose one reason she caught my eye was that the department did not allow children to report with their parents, aunts, uncles, or anyone else. It was allowed on rare occasions, but the attending probation officer had to approve it before the defendant could report. Because of the criminal population that filled our waiting room, children were not permitted in the department. Rapists, murderers, assaulters, sex offenders, and pedophiles, just to name a few, could all be in the waiting room waiting to be seen by their PO's.

This young woman was visibly nervous as she waited in line behind other defendants before passing through the metal detector. I chose to step to the side to watch how this played out. Her turn came up. She handed her diaper bag and purse to the nearest security officer for inspection, and the alarm rang as she pushed the baby stroller through. Security instructed the young mother to remove her baby from the stroller so the stroller could be taken aside for further inspection.

This is where it got weird. She began questioning security, rather loudly, about why she needed to pick up her baby. She didn't want to disturb the baby, who had finally fallen asleep. She was raising her arms in protest, telling the men that she had gotten special permission to bring her baby. The woman demanded to see her officer immediately, and she wanted to know why she was being harassed. People began to take notice of her, and additional men from the security team were called in from across the street. The head of the security team politely approached the woman, taking her aside to try to calm her.

It worked, and the woman finally went to retrieve her baby from the stroller. But before she picked her baby up, she took a deep breath. As she lifted the child, she made sure that a blanket was under the child's bottom. Two security officers escorted the mother and child back through the metal detector. I observed the mother begin to sweat profusely, and the alarm rang immediately upon walking through the detector. The head of security gently took the baby from the mother without issue and patted the baby's backside, revealing a gun in the diaper. I could not believe my eyes. The security officers handcuffed the mother without incident, the gun was collected, and the baby was taken to the Chief's office, awaiting child protective services and EMT to assess the child's health and well-being.

The defendant was there to see a co-worker of mine, and if it had not been for the quick-thinking security team, we might have been one officer short. The young mother was there to kill her probation officer, my colleague, a woman I worked with daily. She was there to kill one of us, and that reality hit hard.

Eventually, the mother was sent to prison for endangerment of a child and conspiracy to commit murder of a court official. The child went on to live with a family member.

B IS FOR BOMB

At approximately 1:00 p.m. on a Friday afternoon, we were getting ready to read the conditions of probation for a new group of defendants who would be arriving from the courthouse at any moment. The other POs and I were located on the second floor, making sure the paperwork was in order. Our supervisor entered the room with panic in her voice, stating that there was potentially a bomb in the building. As we got up to evacuate, the supervisor instructed us to check the trash cans and the boxes under the chairs and tables, stating that if we saw anything suspicious, we were to report it immediately. She quickly exited the room and closed the door. We, of course, began looking for bombs or anything that might resemble one.

What the ever-loving were we doing? We looked. We actually looked. And at some point, we all stopped dead in our tracks, realizing the stupidity of our actions. Glancing at each other without saying a word, we went to the fire escape door located at the back of the room. From the second floor, looking down onto the staff parking lot, we began descending the outdoor stairs. We observed the administration, along with our supervisor, fleeing to their automobiles located in the rear parking lot. *Really*? We knew we weren't respected by the administration, but this was taking that disrespect to a whole new level. We exited the building into the alleyway, a safe distance from the threat, as we watched our boss leave the parking lot, looking at us as they drove right by without concern for our well-being.

We waited for a while, hoping to hear sirens, and hoping the San Antonio police department, which happened to be located just one street over from our building, would come to our aid and send the bomb squad. But nothing. No one came. We eventually went around to the front of the building to see if the police had arrived, but instead we saw several defendants pacing on the sidewalk, murmuring among themselves. "Yeah, man, can't go in, said a bomb might be in there."

Walking through the small crowd that had gathered, we entered the front of the building and found that probation officers were doing as we had earlier, looking for a bomb. We went back to our offices and waited for further instructions. Of course, none was offered, as our so-called supervisors had evacuated. I left the office around 4:00 p.m. to begin a much-needed weekend. The following Monday, nothing was said about the previous Friday, so I asked my supervisor about what had happened. She shrugged her shoulders and laughed.

"Guess it was just a disgruntled defendant calling in a prank," she casually answered me.

My retort was, "Then why did *y'all* leave, asking us to look for the bomb?"

"Look, Pam, if you don't want to be here, you can go find another job!" she scolded me.

Exiting the office, she bumped into me, glaring at me as she stormed past me. I would discover very quickly that if anyone ever questioned the leadership or lack thereof, the reply was "go find another job." My all-time favorite was from one of the assistant chiefs, who would say, "A monkey at the zoo could do this job. We will just find a replacement."

Real professional, *not*! Of course, we, the bitches, stayed on, enduring years of sexual harassment and disrespect, but one great thing that came out of all of this was that we had each other.

COMMUNITY SERVICE, A.K.A. CSR

Defendants placed on probation are required to complete community service (CSR) hours.

These hours must typically be completed within the first few years of probation. Misdemeanor offenders typically receive up to 200 hours of CSR, while felony offenders may receive up to 500 hours.

The philosophy behind CSR is that defendants have taken from society by committing a crime; in return, they must give back by performing duties, chores, or tasks in the community. Sounds harmless enough, doesn't it? Judges and probation officers have had to become very creative in assigning CSR to defendants. Giving back to society is great, but we also want to have an impact on the defendant's lives, hopefully learning something in the process. Occasionally, this would require the PO to be present and witness the defendants completing their CSR hours.

The following are just a few that I witnessed on my caseload:

A young man named Eric, 19, a freshman in college, was driving drunk and wrapped his car around a tree. Eric, the driver, walked away with a few scrapes and bruises, while his best friend since kindergarten was thrown through the front windshield of the car, dying at the scene. Eric was so intoxicated that he passed out, waking up at the hospital handcuffed to the bed, oblivious to what had happened to his friend.

Months passed, and Eric had his day in court. He was sentenced to 10-years probation for intoxication manslaughter and issued 400 hours of community service, plus numerous drug and alcohol treatment classes. Due to Eric's cavalier attitude at his sentencing, the judge came up with an idea for Eric's first 100 hours of CSR. Each month, Eric would place flowers on the graveside of his friend, who was killed because of his negligence. I was required to be present with Eric to make sure this ritual was performed. Because of my crazy weekly work schedule at the probation department and Eric being away at college, we would meet at the cemetery gates on a designated weekend, where I would watch him place flowers on the grave. For the first few months, this task was done in complete silence. Eric never spoke a word and was unable to make eye contact with me. His nonchalant attitude was difficult to watch. He would pull up in his brand-new two-seater Audi convertible without a care in the world. Eric would approach his friend's grave, toss a bouquet of flowers, then walk back to his car, engine still running, with no acknowledgment of my existence, and he would speed off.

During one of our monthly in-person visits, I let Eric know that I was giving up my personal time to be with family and friends once a month so I could meet him at the cemetery to witness the placement of flowers on his friend's grave. I told him that I would appreciate some acknowledgement from him while we are at the cemetery. He stood up, kicked the chair, and pointed his finger at me before walking out and hollering, "Judge said you HAVE to be there, so just deal with it!"

The year was almost over, and we thankfully only had one more time to meet at the cemetery. On this particularly sunny day, I arrived at the gate of the cemetery, but no Eric. I remember being furious, but before I sped off, I noticed a figure on the hill lying next to a grave. It was Eric. Not hearing or seeing me, I approached Eric. He was rocking from side to side in a fetal position, and I heard nonhuman sobbing sounds coming from this young man. I chose to find a nearby bench, sit under a tree, and wait it out. I was equipped with an office 'walkie-talkie' that let me reach a supervisor to tell them about my situation. I requested that Eric's parents be contacted. I knew he was in no shape to drive himself home, nor did I want him to be alone after he left the cemetery.

Approximately 45 minutes later, I saw Eric's parents arrive, and then all three of them knelt by the grave, crying. Knowing that Eric was in the loving arms of his parents, I began to walk away. Behind me, I hear the crunching of the grass and the hard dirt underfoot. Eric was running towards me. He grabbed me and pulled me to the ground. Holding onto each other tightly, both of us in tears, he tried to express his gratitude and remorse, but was unable to form his words. These breakthroughs aren't witnessed very often by probation officers, but I was glad I was there when Eric had his.

Our next few years together went well, and Eric was able to terminate early and has accomplished a lot in his life. He graduated from college in the Carolinas he went on to attend graduate school in California. I even received an invitation to attend his college graduation in North Carolina, but I was unable to attend. I know Eric will remember that day in the cemetery as much as I do. It was a breakthrough for him and an affirming day for me. I am confident I was where I needed to be.

I had a similar situation with another young man. Paul, a 22-two-year-old, was with his college roommate, Adam, and Paul was driving under the influence of alcohol. He was speeding and overcorrected, driving into a ravine. Paul, the driver, passed out at the wheel, and his friend was unconscious at the scene. Paul wakes up in the back of an ambulance while his friend, Adam, is air-lifted to a nearby hospital. Adam suffered a severed spinal cord and was in a coma and was placed on a ventilator. Months passed, and eventually, Adam's parents had to make the decision to place him in a nursing home, as he would never come out of his coma.

Paul took a plea bargain with the prosecutor and was given 5 years of probation for intoxication assault. The judge ordered 200 hours of community service, during which Paul had to report to the nursing home for 4 hours every other Saturday. He was ordered to assist the nursing staff with Adam's needs, reading to him, helping the nursing staff change Adam's sheets, etc. The judge did not require my presence for this stint, which I was grateful for.

Paul was at the nursing facility almost every weekend and holiday, and he went above and beyond what the courts had asked of him. I heard that he was present when Adam's parents decided to remove their only child from the ventilator. I cannot imagine the pain and emotions everyone in that room must have felt, but I bet it was the most difficult thing Paul will ever experience.

I don't know what happened to Paul, since he had requested that his probation be transferred to another county so he could finish college. I did, however, receive a letter from the nursing home director enclosing a note that Paul had written to Adam. The director thought it was important that I read the letter. The nurse's aide found the letter in the pillowcase of Adam's bed on the day he died. In the letter, Paul apologized for taking his life from him and told him how much he enjoyed having him as a friend and a roommate. He cited memories of fraternity parties, football games, and girls they had met. Paul confessed in the letter that he had become a better person, saying he hadn't touched a drop of alcohol since the night of the crash. He stated he would live his life for Adam and be the best possible man he could be. Many lives were changed and touched because of Paul's actions. It's sad that sometimes it takes a horrific event to change our ways.

Here are some other examples of community service:

Some defendants gifted their athletic abilities to help at the local YMCA. One young man on my caseload loved basketball, and he was good at it. He asked if he could complete his community service hours by forming and coaching girls' and boys' basketball teams that would eventually compete against other YMCA clubs. It became a huge success! He was instrumental in helping troubled youth build confidence and in teaching kids to be leaders. Both the community and the defendant benefit from projects like these.

I had a woman who was a beautician, so for her community service, she offered to cut hair at homeless shelters. Her love of community and willingness to give had such an impact on the shelter.

A veterinarian also worked with a homeless shelter, providing free vaccinations for the pets of the homeless. Another great win!

One of the first things I would ask a defendant who was placed on my caseload was what they thought their biggest gift or talent was. I would then try to help them help me come up with creative ways to perform community service. Something they would enjoy while making others happy. I hope this movement continues.

SAN ANTONIO OR BUST!

This chapter provides a bit about me before I became a probation officer.

I was excited to get home and have dinner with my husband, anticipating a decadent meal at our favorite French bistro. I was more excited because our marital relationship was in desperate need of some romantic zhzusching.

Paxton, my *practice* hubby, had called twice during the day to secure our dinner date. He closed our last conversation by saying he loved me. He *never* said he loved me, and in fact, I can only remember a handful of times he was verbally affectionate towards me during our 10 years together.

Our wedding day wasn't any different. He used his code of *1, 2, 3* upon exchanging our vows, followed by a wink and a smile. His *1, 2, 3* code was his way of saying he loved me. After seven years of dating, Paxton, or Prince Paxton as his mommy called him, finally proposed. It took him seven years because he knew I was about to seek relationships elsewhere.

"I don't want to lose you, let's get married!" he exclaimed.

In retrospect, it was a bad decision at best. I shouldn't have married Paxton; he wasn't the marrying kind. I just wish he had the balls to tell me beforehand. He liked to prowl for women, and it was a true "sport" for Pax and some of his buddies. This so-called sport, however, continued well into our marriage. A look at his formative pre-adult years indicated what kind of person Pax was. It should have been a huge alarm that would render someone like me deaf. I chose to turn a deaf ear and ignore it during our dating years, and for a short while, after we married.

Pax and his pals formed a club in college called the *PIG PATROL*, which was an institution formed when Pax joined a fraternity in an Ivy League school back East. The private college population was small and elite, and the women-to-men ratio was skewed at this higher institute of learning, making the hunt for women more challenging. A polo shirt with a pig emblazoned on the left side was the dress code for Saturday evening for the frat boys. One of the events enjoyed by the pigs would be to go forth into the community or a sorority, pick an unsuspecting *victim*, and liquor up the young lady just enough to get her back to the frat house. The *victim* would then be escorted to the fraternity's living room, where another brother would be nearby with a camera, taking photos of this poor girl with her date for the evening.

Here is the caveat: the winner of the night's events was voted on by other fraternity members, and the prize would go to the pig that brought home the ugliest girl. The girls' photos would eventually be hung on a wall of shame in the basement pledge room, behind a large wooden door. The hideous and sad truth about this game is that its continuation went well into my husband's adult life, influencing his pathetic friends, married or single. It was a black cloud in an already tumultuous marriage.

Coming home on Central Expressway, in the Dallas metroplex, was an adventure. The drive was typically stressful, but I was in such a great mood. I was anxious to begin my night alone with Pax, yearning for this reconnection for quite some time. The evening commute wasn't going to deter my eagerness and excitement to get home to what I thought was going to be a memorable evening. As it turns out, it would be memorable, but not in the way I had been anticipating it. It was instead a pivotal moment in my mere 27 years on this earth—an evening I will never forget.

Walking into our recently purchased 100-plus-year-old home was such a joy. The home had character with old-world charm oozing from the moment you walked in. The foyer displayed an antique round occasional table and a large vase of fresh flowers, delivered weekly by my hubby. The vibrant colors and aroma of sweetness never disappointed. The hardwood floors creaked underfoot with each step. I often wondered about the previous owners who inhabited the house. Where did they place the Christmas tree? What meals did they eat in the opium den style cloth-covered walled dining room? Were there children who lived there? Our family's heirloom antiques fit beautifully in the rooms and appeared as if they had been in the house since it was built in the early nineteen hundreds.

The daily routine ensued: checking the mail, letting our golden retrievers, Pavlov and Einstein, out for their early-evening romp, and their daily terrorizing of the squirrels and birds in our large, fenced backyard.

Starting up the stairs to our second-floor bedroom, I stopped dead in my tracks at a most disgusting sight. A used condom lay on the first staircase landing. A used condom, on *my* floor, in *my* house, that *my* parents so generously paid the down payment on at seventeen percent interest. A thousand visuals swam in my head. I became physically ill as the images flooded my mind, my heart racing, and my blood pressure rose through the roof as I began to sob uncontrollably. I knew Pax had been unfaithful in the past; it was an unspoken part of a very non-traditional marriage, of which I had had enough. He did not want a monogamous relationship with me, and I knew from the fourth year of our courtship that I should've run and run as fast as I could. But woulda, coulda, shoulda, live and learn. (Thanks, Wesley T, for being there for me when I fell). Paxton equated sex as a form of entertainment, and if I wanted to be a part of his life, then I would endure this desire he had. The desire for other women. He assured me that there were never emotional ties with these women; it was just sex. I was the lucky one, *ha*, the one he would have the emotional bond with. As a couple, there were rules I asked him to respect. Absolutely *no* women were ever allowed into our home for his sexual tryst, and if he was going to be out all night, no questions allowed, because his brutal honesty was more than I could bear.

At 7:30 p.m., the moon was slowly rising on this February evening, and the light from the moon was shining through the staircase landing window, illuminating the used condom lying on the floor, giving off a translucent glow. The ringing of the den phone thrust me out of the strange trance and back into reality. It was Pax on the receiving end, and by his slurred words, I could tell that he had started our romantic evening without me. I could hear glasses clinking in the background as well as a woman's laughter. He was with friends, celebrating his recent win of a huge settlement in a civil case. A case that had taken up three years of our lives. At that moment, I instantly knew how little I meant to him. I was not the one celebrating with him; he was with his pigs.

Being married to a prominent attorney had its pros and cons, including late work hours, entertaining clients, travel, stressful depositions, motions, but most importantly, the ego. Pax had graduated at the top of his law class from a prestigious law school back East. Upon graduation, he moved to Dallas, Texas, to escape the gloomy and cold weather. He had also heard that Texas women were the prettiest in all the United States. The day I met Pax, I was moving boxes down a flight of stairs from my condo, and he had recently purchased the condo next door to mine. Oddly enough, seven years later, I would marry the boy next door.

Pax was raised in New Haven, Connecticut, by two adoring parents and two older sisters. His dad was a genius consultant and a professor at Yale. Pax's mom had graduated from Wellesley College and possessed a degree in homemaking. She was a tireless volunteer who refused to be wrapped up in the trappings of the snobbish lifestyle surrounding her in the Connecticut community. Pax's two sisters were overachievers as well, but his entire family welcomed me with open arms. The only criticisms they had for me were my Texas drawl, being a Southern Baptist, and, oh, I was a Republican.

Pax told me he wasn't coming home till later because of excessive partying, and he was leaving the bar to head over to Graham's, an initiated pig man himself. They were going to have pizza and watch some stupid sports thing on TV.

"What about our night out?" I asked.

He was cavalier in his response, brushing me off and alluding to the fact that we may or may not have dinner later in the week if he wasn't too busy. Before I could make mention of the ill-fated item on my staircase, he hung up the phone. I was furious and unable to calm myself.

I turned on the stereo and started petting Pavlov and Einstein, trying to soothe my anxious thoughts. I then walked downstairs to get the pooch's dinner, stepping over the condom still on the staircase landing.

Instantly, a rush of energy and anger took over my body as if I had no control over my actions. I changed into jeans and a Dallas Cowboys sweatshirt (this was a time when the Dallas Cowboys were good), slipped into my unlaced tennis shoes, and retrieved the condom using an unsharpened pencil, maneuvering it ever so delicately, allowing the latex to rest limply over the pencil.

I raced down the second flight of stairs while gingerly holding the pencil, not to disturb the condom. I made sure the dog's bowl was full of fresh water, then I activated the house alarm and sprinted out the back door toward the garage. I fidgeted with my car keys to unlock my car, never dropping the pencil. Quite a feat, I admit.

My Saab had a five-speed stick shift, and I needed both hands to drive and shift, so I set the pencil and condom on top of my coffee cup, which was still in the cup holder. Yuck, but it worked. I was grateful that Graham only lived a few miles away, so I would not have to traverse any highways. Getting out of the car with the pencil-laden condom was easier than I had anticipated.

As I approached Graham's front door, I noticed the door was ajar. I could hear a loud, obnoxious female laughing over some sports event on the television. I peered through the front door and saw Pax, Graham, and a tall, buxom blonde seated on the couch, watching TV.

A delivery guy from Campisi's pizza was getting out of the delivery truck when I grabbed the pizza from him as he was reaching to ring the doorbell. I walked into the house carrying one of Campisi's specials. All three were shocked to see me holding the hot pizza box while the delivery dude was on my heels, demanding the pizza back.

"Lady, you're going to have to pay for that."

I gave the biggest *eat shit and die* look to the poor guy who had no idea what he had walked into. Before the fab three could formulate any words, I took the used condom resting ever so delicately on the pencil, and with very little effort, I placed the hot pizza box on the coffee table, opened the lid of the box, and tossed the used condom into the air.

The five of us watched in slow motion as the condom landed smack dab in the middle of the Campesis's *All the Way* specialty square-shaped pizza. A culinary sin had just been committed for which my penitence will never be paid. I took the pencil that the condom had made its home on for the last thirty minutes and *stabbed* the condom into the pizza. No one spoke a word. We all glanced at each other, and the pizza guy threw his hands up in the air and exclaimed, "Really, lady?!"

Pax and my eyes locked in an eerie glare. I didn't yell or scream, I simply turned and walked out the front door towards the car. I had an indescribable feeling, one that I had never experienced before. All I know is that it was one of the most defining moments in my life, and one that I still look back on with great fondness.

The blonde woman started chasing me, and Graham, Pax, and the pizza dude were in tow. This woman, as it turns out, was an 'exotic dancer', a.k.a. stripper extraordinaire, and worked at a gentleman's club that the pigs often frequented. She was very apologetic, trying to explain that the condom was hers, and she swore on her grandmother's grave that she and Pax didn't engage in sex at my house.

"Graham and I got it on!" she declared.

I turned to all four of them and asked, "Was there *nowhere else* that you and Graham could have had sex? Hmmmm... maybe here at Graham's house instead of mine?"

She looked befuddled, and then her light bulb went off as if to say in her pea-brain mind, that could have been a possibility.

"*Why* didn't you throw the condom into the trash? *Why* leave it for *me* to find on the staircase landing?"

To this day, I don't want to know what happened that day, but it's no longer important to me.

By the time I finished my rant, I was in the car, ignition on, car shifted in reverse, backing out onto the street, and back to the house. The house that I would no longer call home. Pax was speechless, and as I dove off, my last image of him was standing alone in the dust. I couldn't get home fast enough to start packing. My life in Big D was over.

That February evening was the night I decided that I could no longer live the lifestyle that Pax had chosen for us. Going forward, I would make my own decisions, even if that meant living my life alone. I rang my favorite Aunt and Uncle, who lived in San Antonio, to see if I could stay with them for a while until I made my next life choice. I started packing up our fine China, Baccarat crystal, and silver that were treasured wedding gifts. When I look back on this, I should have just packed my clothes and toothbrush and gotten the hell out of there, but those items represented something to me. I crammed as much of my life with Pax as I could in that four-door, hatchback Saab.

Around 3:00 a.m. I realized I was too exhausted to make the five-hour drive to San Antonio, so I curled up on the couch downstairs with Pavlov and Einstein by my side, and cried myself to sleep. I awoke to the sun shining through our beautiful stained-glass window and the loving licks of the two dogs. I revisited the events of the prior evening and began psyching myself up to say goodbye to the two precious golden faces looking at me, their tails wagging, clueless about what had transpired the night before.

My last motherly act for Pavlov and Einstein was to give them fresh water from the outdoor faucet and to leave an extra treat in their food bowls. Not able to look into the loving four brown eyes, I sprinted through the kitchen door, through the formal foyer, setting the house alarm one last time, out the front door, and into my car. Tears were streaming down my face, and I could barely see to drive.

I purposefully did not look back at the house for fear I would turn around and stay—stay in a life that I could no longer be a part of. Pax never came home that night, and to this day, he still can't believe that I left.

[Sidebar: if you have never been to Campisi's Italian Restaurant, established in 1946, on Mockingbird Lane, located in Dallas, Texas, it is a must. I don't usually care for the cheesy, doughy

culinary fare, but Campisi's is amazing!!!! The "All the Way" square pizza is something to enjoy before leaving this earth. Their pasta doesn't suck either.]

Leaving my job in Dallas wasn't difficult, but my boss was furious that I left without giving a month's notice, as the company required. He was, however, cooperative and understood why I left so abruptly.

I cried all the way from Dallas to San Antonio, about 5 hours non-stop. I loved living in Dallas, with its museums, restaurants, shopping, culture, ballet, and symphony. I hated the country club scene; the people were fake, pretentious, and snobby, but I had met some wonderful people through my junior league connection. I also left behind friends from my hometown, as well as fraternity brothers and dear girlfriends I had met from my Waco days at Baylor University, about a couple of hours south of Big D. I had spent 10 years making Dallas my home.

Starting over was scary, but an exciting new life awaited me. I just couldn't see it yet, consumed by sadness. I remember driving up to my aunt and uncle's house, arriving at dusk. The lights from inside their large, two-story, Tudor home gave off a warm, inviting glow. My aunt and uncle had lived all over the United States as my uncle was in sales. This afforded my family fun summers visiting New York, Virginia, Missouri, and Michigan before they made San Antonio home.

I was greeted by their golden retriever named Bexar (after the county), and by Gus, a *roadside* retriever who was a mid-sized lab mix rescue dog. Both offered loads of licks and much-needed love that I welcomed. Aunt Paula ushered me to their beautiful backyard, which would later explode with Texas wildflowers. Still cold in February, the protected patio was warmed by a fire going in the chimenea that Uncle was stoking. Excited to see each other, we hugged and caught up on the day's events.

Exhausted, I fell asleep in a soft, fluffy lounge chair listening to the sounds of the flowing water from the outdoor water feature that flowed into a beautiful, small pond. Uncle gently woke me up, stating barbecue and a cold bottle of wine were on the dining table. I wasn't hungry, but knew I needed to eat something, so I grabbed my uncle's hand as he helped me up. We walked tandem into the house for supper.

After our leisurely meal, I unpacked my car, filled with wedding gifts, and placed them in the garage. I had the entire upstairs to myself, as both of my cousins were adults and no longer lived in San Antonio; three bedrooms and a large bath were at my disposal. I settled in, called mom and dad in Lubbock to let them know I had arrived safely. Now what? Sleep that night came easily for me, since it had been an emotional day. The next day was going to be *the first day of the rest of my life!* For the first time, I understood the true meaning of that statement.

The next day, I showered, dressed in a suit, and drove to downtown San Antonio to drop off my resume at the Bexar County Adult Probation Department. I had an interview within the week and was invited to volunteer for the department for a few weeks. This unpaid 'volunteer' time was set up to vet both the prospective employee and the employer. I was hired on the last day of my volunteer time, and told to report to work the following Monday, and my formal training would begin then.

I was the first of the "bitches" to join the Bexar County Adult Probation Department, and had no idea of the life and journey I was about to embark upon. Knowing what I know now, I would do the whole thing over again.

BRUNETTE FROM BOISER

Enter *Bitch number two...*

Clickity, clack, clickity, clack, clack, clack! White high heels echoing off the linoleum floors, fading into my office space, followed by a voice.

"Hi, I'm Valerie, you can call me Val."

She dropped a file onto my already disheveled desk, adding to my pile, and without a smile, she turned and walked out. *Whoa, attitude* with a capital A, but I knew I loved this girl from the minute she said hi.

Val stood barely five feet tall, weighing in at ninety pounds wet. She was a brunette with a curly, big Texas coif (the higher the hair, the closer to God), wearing a white suit with maroon pantyhose—yes, maroon pantyhose—and white high-heeled shoes. A difficult design choice, but somehow it worked on Val.

I had just returned from a weeklong holiday when Val had blessed me with her presence, so we had not been formally introduced. Val's husband had recently been promoted, prompting a move from Uvalde to San Antonio, a community about 45 minutes up the road. The population of Uvalde in the early 1990's was 14,800, and the population in San Antonio was 998,000. Talk about culture shock! Val was already a certified adult probation officer, so we were lucky to have her expertise. She taught me a great deal, mainly how to laugh again and not put up with anybody's guff, a.k.a., shit. Having the gift of gab, Val could talk the paint off a wall. She was articulate, intelligent, cute as a button, and *sassy!*

LASSY FROM LAREDO

Bitch number three... hailed from Laredo, Texas. "Nuts" had attended college at the University of Incarnate Word in San Antonio, so she was already familiar with the lay of the land. She was urged to join our little family by a friend with whom she had grown up in Laredo. Her friend was already a misdemeanor probation officer and had been with the department for a short while.

On the day of Nuts' arrival, she entered county court number nine as if she had been working here her entire life. Personable, friendly, and exuberant doesn't begin to describe her. She is like a female Roy Rogers—never met a stranger. Her positive attitude radiated like her blonde hair, which resembled a lion's mane, thick, golden, and flowy. (I am still jealous of this bitch's hair). She was wearing a yellow suit with matching heels; her choice of yellow matched her personality. Nuts' best quality has always been her laughter and joy of living, and you could hear her laughing from across the street. And no, it's not even annoying, but rather downright contagious. If you're in a foul mood, it won't take you long to be in a good mood if Nuts is around. This woman will laugh you out of your funk.

SAVVY AND SASSY
FROM SAN ANTONE

Bitch number four... is the only one of the originals who was born and bred in San Antonio, (a.k.a. San Antone) Texas. I don't think I have ever met a person as quippy and clever as Diane. She can pivot and turn on a dime, matching the most educated individual's repartee without any hesitation. She isn't intimidated by the most ferocious of attorneys, and it was a true joy watching her in court as she defended her PSIs (Pre-Sentence Investigation reports).

Diane's grandfather, a retired police officer, shared his love of the law, which sparked her interest in earning a criminal justice degree from Southwest Texas State (now known as Texas State). Hired straight out of college in the early 1990s, she and another woman were two of the youngest ever to be employed as probation officers in Bexar County.

Diane has a love for music, rock, and country, knowing every word of every song. Her big brown eyes hover over her intoxicating smile, followed by a great laugh. Diane has the gift of meeting people through her great sense of humor. She is not a forgettable person, and once you meet her, you won't forget her. Diane knows people from all over, so it seems that almost every time we go out, even today, we run into someone who knows her. On vacation, we were on a cruise, and wouldn't you know it, smack dab in the middle of the Caribbean, strolling on deck B, we hear, "Diane." Just another admirer she had known from school.

Diane loves learning and has earned two graduate degrees while working full-time—a feat I admire. She continues to evolve and share herself through her job and volunteering.

Something that all of us bitches have in common besides our jobs is our families, and they are incredibly important to each of us. All our families share our commitment to leading a life of service. Our parents raised each of us with the philosophy that we were put on this earth to pay it forward.

Family, faith, and friendship sprinkled with a wicked sense of humor. Not a bad way to walk through this life.

THURSDAY NIGHT THERAPY

Our workload at the department was intense, and because we had to work on Fridays, we would get together each Thursday night at one of our homes. Potluck would be the food fare, as each of us would bring our favorite casserole, snacks, dips, and chips, along with someone assigned to the dessert, which would round out what we called a perfect evening. (My casserole that was easy to make and loved by all was my chicken spaghetti. Comfort food at its best, and still a fan favorite.

Thursday night rang in a much-needed good old-fashioned giggle fest. *NO BOYFRIENDS OR HUSBANDS ALLOWED!* Dinner was enjoyed earlier before the television was turned on, discussing the present week's shenanigans, the cases that we had heard in court or the office bull shit, as well as the ever-popular girl gossip. We also shared the people who had played a part in the week's craziness, whether it be a defendant or one of our colleagues at the office. We would catch up on how our families were doing and how we were doing, and if we needed to talk about something, this was OUR therapy.

After dinner and therapy, the Thursday night *must-see* TV lineup was our go-to, which included the following shows:

Will & Grace, Seinfeld, Mad About You, Friends, Frasier, and the evening ended with the one-hour medical drama, *ER.* All amazing TV shows, and most are still in syndication with a new generation of followers. At the conclusion of *ER,* we would grab our dishes from the potluck, hug one another, and head home to get a good night's sleep, already looking forward to next week's Thursday night therapy.

DEFENDANT VS. HAPPY HOUR

Sherlock's, a local San Antonio bar, had a reasonable happy hour, a nice ambiance, and, more importantly, a great DJ and a decent dance floor. Diane also knew a group of young men from her high school days who would play live music there. The band is still together, making music and living their best lives.

Occasionally, the bitches and I would treat ourselves to a Friday happy hour after a long work week. We'd order drinks, find a table near the dance floor, and wait for the next fun song so we could shake our groove thing (no dance partners needed; group dancing was more fun!). Between songs, we would share more stories that had not been covered the previous night at Thursday night therapy, and there were always stories.

One night, Diane and I began dancing on the crowded dance floor when I bumped into a young man. He spilt his cold, icy drink down my back. Gasping, I turned to apologize to this person whom I immediately recognized. Stan was one of my defendants on my caseload for an intoxication assault.

Stan and his friend were speeding down Highway 281 when he spun out of control and hit a telephone pole. His friend was pinned in the car and sustained a broken leg. Stan was not supposed to be in a bar, let alone drinking.

Our eyes locked, and when he realized who I was, his eyes lit up like fireworks on the Fourth of July. He tried to run off the dance floor, but I was able to grab his arm, his drink still in his possession. I noticed a San Antonio police officer providing security at the bar's front door, so I guided the defendant to the door and told the officer of our plight. He detained Stan until I located his friends to let them know that I would be sending their friend home for the evening. I took the drink from him, making sure it was alcohol, and called a cab. The police officer made sure the cab driver took him straight home. The following Monday, I had to draft a motion to revoke, citing the actions by the defendant.

A few days later, we were in court before the judge, where I recommended more treatment. I included reporting four times a month instead of one, and having the defendant take a drug called Antabuse. Antabuse would be administered by the medical staff three times a week. If a person drinks alcohol while taking this drug, it makes them violently ill, vomiting till your clavicle hurts. Antabuse is designed to reshape a defendant's thinking for alcohol consumption, in hopes the defendant will no longer want to drink, at least while they are under the supervision of probation.

Words of wisdom: *DON'T DRINK AND DRIVE*. You never know who you will run into.

The Texas Penal Code defines Intoxication Assault, in the context of Texas Law, as the act of causing serious bodily injury to another person while operating a motor vehicle or other vehicle (like a boat or aircraft) in a public place while intoxicated. It is a more serious form of Driving While Intoxicated (DWI), where intoxication leads to a serious injury.

The Texas Penal Code, Chapter 49.07

JUST A BIT LOUDER NOW

Phu, a young, quiet, respectful, unassuming man from Vietnam, along with his young wife, came to our fair city to attend graduate school at the University of Texas at San Antonio (*Go Roadrunners!*). Phu and his wife had not been in America very long and were unaware of our traditions and customs, let alone the law. Phu and his wife were in their apartment when they had gotten into a heated argument, so heated that the neighbors called the police. When the police arrived, they found Phu's wife with a bloody face and torn clothes. Phu was arrested on assault charges, eventually being granted 2 years of misdemeanor probation, thus bringing him onto my caseload.

After introducing myself and asking him his first question, it became very apparent that Phu had no idea what I was saying. He did not speak a drop of English, and I didn't speak a drop of Vietnamese. So, this is how stupid I was: I continued to interview Phu, but instead of using my normal voice, I began to shout because surely he would understand my louder, obnoxious Texas twang in English, right? Wrong!

I began shouting, "IN THIS COUNTRY WE DO NOT HIT."

Phu just sat there dazed, unable to communicate. I immediately called the court to get a translator over to my office asap, as I was making a fool of myself. My colleagues in the surrounding offices were laughing hysterically, and poor Phu was just confused and quietly afraid of this crazed mad woman yelling at him.

It didn't take long for the translator to arrive, and she was very apologetic. She was to report with Phu on this day to translate, but she mixed up the dates. Phu was now pacing in my small office, screaming at this translator. I am sure he was describing what had transpired between the two of us, and I am betting it wasn't favorable.

The translator did get Phu to calm down when she explained to me that he was very confused as to why he was on probation and why the police came and arrested him. The translator continued to tell me that in his country, depending on the families' norms, wives were sometimes considered property, and he could beat her if he so desired. If she didn't obey him, he could even kill her, femicide, sometimes without consequence (According to Merriam-Webster dictionary, the term femicide, noun, was first introduced to our vernacular in 1976; it means the gender-based murder of a woman or girl by a man). Welcome to America, buddy, and even worse, welcome to Texas, where women are revered.

The next few months with Phu were not pleasant, since he obviously didn't like a woman telling him what to do; he had a female judge, a female translator, and a female probation officer. Talk about a great episode for the *Twilight Zone*.

Phu, along with his translator, reported each month like clockwork, but Phu had failed to show up for his anger management class, hadn't started any of his community service hours, and, to make matters worse, he and his wife were not going to court-mandated marriage counseling.

Arriving at my office after a fun weekend, I began reading the daily arrest reports, and lo and behold, Phu's name jumped off the page like a lightning bolt. Phu had been arrested for assaulting his wife again, but this time he was arrested for assault with a deadly weapon, which is a felony. The police report stated that Phu and his wife had gotten into a physical fight, and the weapon of choice was a baseball bat. He had broken her jaw, broken three of her ribs, choked her out, and thrown her across the room so hard that her head left an indentation in the sheetrock, rendering her unconscious. Neighbors again called the police, and Phu's wife was rushed to the hospital, where she was in a coma. Bail had been denied for Phu.

Upon contacting the translator to inform her that she wouldn't need to attend our next scheduled appointment, she stated she wasn't surprised to hear of Phu's arrest. She said she knew that Phu was unhappy, homesick, and just not fitting in. He felt he was losing control of his wife while she was thriving, doing well in grad school, learning English, making friends, and enjoying her new life in Texas.

A few months later, we would be before the judge on a motion to revoke Phu's probation. During this hearing, the prosecutor, Phu's defense attorney, Phu's translator, Phu, and I were the players in this scenario—no jurors. The Judge, with the probation officer's help, has the final say on what will happen to the defendant. Friends, family, and witnesses may be called by the prosecutor and the defense attorney to testify.

Before the court proceedings began, I met Phu's wife along with her college sponsor. Bluish and greenish bruises lingered around her sweet, soulful, and trusting eyes, still healing from the trauma she had experienced a few months earlier. Her jaw was wired shut, making it difficult for her to speak. She told me she had not returned to school, but she was looking forward to going back for the summer semester. I was seated next to Phu's wife when the holding cell door opened, and three bailiffs escorted Phu, donning the orange bilious jail uniform, leg shackles, and handcuffs. Without notice, Phu's wife grabbed my arm, an audible gasp escaped from her wired shut mouth, and I could feel that she was petrified. Her college sponsor wrapped her arms around her, and I held her hand.

Phu was planted in a chair located in the jury box along with the other prisoners awaiting to be heard on that same day. He was not cooperative, as he was isolated from the other prisoners; three bailiffs flanked him for his protection and that of the other prisoners. Phu was visibly agitated, and when he looked up, he saw me, his wife, and the college sponsor. Three women again. I am beginning to see a theme here. Phu stood and began yelling something that I, of course, didn't understand, but it upset Phu's wife as she squeezed my arm very tightly. The bailiffs pushed Phu into the wooden chair so hard that the leg shackles echoed against the wood, demanding silence from the defendant as the court bailiff entered, announcing, "All rise."

Thankfully, our case would be heard first due to Phu's agitation. Shaky and breathing abnormally, I approached the bench along with Phu's translator. I knew Phu was handcuffed, shackled, and heavily guarded, but I was still scared. I had little to no moisture in my mouth, and when the judge asked me a question, I tried to speak, but the words wouldn't come. The judge saw I was distressed, so she poured a cup of water, stood, and handed it to me over the bench. I chugged the water and regained my composure.

"Your honor, we are here today for a motion to revoke, citing a new assault with a deadly weapon…"

I had my mojo back, and I was able to articulate the new charge. The judge asked that Phu's wife approach. I asked the judge if she could be seated on the witness stand so she would not be near her estranged husband, and she allowed it. The judge and the prosecutor asked her questions as she showed photos of herself in the hospital. The judge's eyes widened as she looked at the colored photos revealing the trauma that Phu's wife had endured. The neighbors also came to testify on the victim's behalf. Phu's defense attorney did not ask any questions. Phu was sneering and speaking quietly under his breath, rolling his eyes with each person's testimony, shuffling with the sound of metal handcuffs with each shift of his feet. The case took up most of the morning as everything said had to be translated to Phu via the translator.

After hearing all the witnesses, the judge had reached a decision. Phu would be sent back to Vietnam, and he would never be allowed back into the United States.

"Prosecutor, please contact immigration to begin this process as soon as possible. Court will be in recess, and we will resume after lunch."

The bailiff announced, "All rise."

I immediately went to Phu's wife, making sure she understood everything that had happened, reminding her that immigration would be sending Phu back to Vietnam. She was trembling, and I tried to reassure her that things would be all right. I let her know that she could remain in Texas on a school visa. She told me that when Phu was yelling at her earlier, he was telling her that she had shamed her family and that her life was now in danger.

Puzzled, I didn't understand. She explained to me that she would never be allowed to see her family again, as she had embarrassed them back home; her father and brothers might possibly come for her. I looked into the college sponsors' eyes for some reassurance that things would be ok, but I didn't get that feeling. I suddenly felt deflated and defeated. One problem was solved, but now a bigger one had arisen. What would the wife's future bring?

My takeaway from this case would be a selfish one at best. I was never prouder to be an American woman, and a bonus, a Texas woman. I am respected, I have a voice, and I am listened to. I may not always be heard, but at least I can speak my opinion. Women here are allowed to go to school, work, own a business, own land, and vote. The world is our oyster, and if we put the hard work in, we can do anything we want. Yes, I took these things for granted, and yes, I am aware that other countries do not afford the same freedoms for women that I have. *Thankfully*, things for women are changing. It might be slow, but changes are happening all over the world in the twenty-first century.

GOD BLESS AMERICA, AND GOD BLESS TEXAS!

"LEAD US NOT INTO TEMPTATION…"

As we know, in the United States, the legal drinking age to consume alcohol is twenty-one. This was the early 1990s, and in San Antonio, some townie or local bars would sometimes allow underage drinking for individuals serving our country—people in the military.

Dan, a 19-year-old, had just recently completed a ten-week, three-phase Army boot camp at Fort Knox, located in the beautiful Bluegrass State of Kentucky. Returning to San Antonio for the Thanksgiving holiday season and a much needed two weeks leave, Dan and some of his friends found their way Saturday evening to the neighborhood watering hole. As Dan was enjoying a cold brew and a competitive game of pool, Beatrice a.k.a. Bea, approached Dan with two beers in her hands.

"Hey, I'm Bea."

Dan was smitten from her first word. Bea was not much of a conversationalist, but at 5'6", thin, with hazel eyes, blonde, and beautiful, she didn't need to say much. Upon meeting Bea, Dan said his world just stopped, and he knew his life would never be the same. Boy, it never was.

After his leave, Dan was sent to Kuwait to fight in the first Gulf War in the early 90s, leaving his newfound love behind. Letters were written between the two over the next year while Dan was deployed. The Gulf War lasted only 42 days, with a seven-month U.S. occupation, so a reunion between the two was sooner rather than later.

When Dan returned to San Antonio, he called Bea and said he wished to meet her parents. If he was going to court her, he wanted to be a true Texas gentleman and ask her parents for permission to date their daughter. Dan was even more in love than he had remembered. He did all the right things. Bea met Dan's folks, who also gave their blessing to the relationship. Dan saw Bea every night before he was to report to Fort Leonard Wood in Missouri to begin his training to become an MP (Military Police). He was falling in love, hard and fast. Dan made the decision to abstain from sex until he met the girl he was going to marry. Not only was Dan a patriot, but he was a chivalrous man raised in the Catholic faith.

Dan attended MP training and spent approximately nine months in Missouri. Bea's parents brought her up for a long weekend during his training so they could see each other. This is the weekend that Dan decided to ask Bea to marry him. Beyond thrilled, Bea and her mother set about making wedding plans immediately upon returning to Texas. Dan made a special request for leave to go home to San Antonio to get his grandmother's engagement ring and present it to Bea.

Dan proposed again, this time at a fancy downtown restaurant located on the romantic San Antonio River Walk. After dinner, Dan had booked a beautiful hotel room so that he and Bea could spend an amorous evening together, this being the first time that they would make love. Everything was going great until Dan took Bea home the next morning. He was greeted by a very angry father, who wanted to know why he had kept Bea out all night. Upset, Dan stated that he thought everything was all right since they had just gotten engaged, and marriage was forthcoming. What was the big deal? Bea's father instructed Dan to leave the premises immediately, and then he took his daughter to the nearest hospital to have a rape kit performed; semen was present.

The next day, two San Antonio police officers arrived at Dan's parents' house. Dan was arrested, citing aggravated sexual assault of a child, a.k.a. rape, against his new fiancée. At the Bexar County jail, the magistrate read the arrest charge to Dan, and it was the first time he heard how old Bea was. She was only 14-years-old.

"FOURTEEN? FOURTEEN? A CHILD?" Dan kept repeating out loud to the magistrate. *"NO…*there is no way my fiancé is fourteen."

It suddenly occurred to Dan that when he met Bea, she would have been just a mere 13-years-old. He became physically ill and was escorted to the nearest restroom, accompanied by two sheriff's deputies. Crying uncontrollably and throwing up, Dan began to realize the serious amount of trouble he was in. The questions were circling in his head faster than he could process any logical answers. Bea approached *him* at the bar. Why or how could she even get into the bar at that age?

Her parents had sanctioned the relationship and were excited about the engagement. Dan had even seen her Texas photo driver's license showing she was eighteen. How on God's green earth had she gotten a driver's license so young? It was a fake ID. *Duh!* In the state of Texas, the age of consent to have sex is seventeen, not fourteen, even if the person is a willing participant; that is the law.

Dan's parents posted bond after he spent over 24 hours in jail due to the long processing procedures. Dan's mom cried the entire car ride home, and his dad was speechless, confused, and befuddled. How could this happen to his son? I am sure you, as the reader, have just as many questions as I did when I first came to know this case.

Well, Beatrice's parents encouraged her and her sister to dress up and go to the local bar on weekends, since there were a lot of military men there. They wanted the girls to find a husband who could provide a good life for them. Being married to a husband in the military meant they could travel, see the world, and get free housing if they lived on base. Medical coverage would also be available to them.

Both Bea and her sister were no longer attending school, and they were only sixth- and seventh-grade educated. Mom taught the girls how to dress and look older by the way they applied their makeup, and she also taught them the art of flirting.

Dan would have been Bea's parents' dream guy, or so I thought. The goal they had set for their girls was coming to fruition. I am still in a quandary as to why Bea's dad became so enraged that fateful Sunday morning.

The day arrived for Dan's case, and he was charged with aggravated sexual assault of a child and granted 10 years of felony probation. Dan was dishonorably discharged from the Army and was unemployed. He would also have to register as a sex offender, and will now and forever be known as a sex offender. Dan had to move in with his parents, as apartment complexes do not allow sex offenders to take up residence where children are living.

This title was also branded on his driver's license. A placard must be placed in the front window of a sex offender's home stating that a known registered sex offender resides in this location. A bumper sticker must be placed on the automobile that you drive stating that a sex offender is driving this automobile, and listing the probation office's phone number. The neighbors are notified via mail that they are living near or next to a sex offender.

After the 10-year probation term is completed, the defendant will have to continue reporting to the local sex offender program authorities for the remainder of their *life*!!! The defendant will not be able to leave the county in which they are registered, so hunker down. I hope you love the town you have been charged in, because more than likely, you won't be able to leave. All travel outside of the county must be approved by the court. You're not allowed to live near a school, and you cannot go to any public places where children might be in attendance, such as amusement parks, concerts, theatre, etc. The defendant must attend many classes and pay fines and fees to the courts.

I want to stress that I believe in the law and in justice, but in this case, I am not sure justice was served. Dan did everything right throughout this relationship, in my humble opinion, so why was HE being punished? I think Bea's parents should be locked away for the rest of their days. I feel they were the ones at fault.

Through job counseling, we were able to find Dan a good-paying construction job. He tried to attend college, but higher education institutions wouldn't admit him due to his felony conviction. Dan completed his probation without incident and never complained about his circumstances.

As the law dictates, Dan remains on the Texas sex registration list still today. He continued to live with his parents until he married. He is married with two children and is probably a grandfather by now. He married Bea. Yes, he married the love of his life, the girl he was smitten with from the first *"Hey!"*

TO *BE*lieve OR NOT *BE*lieve

A man named Owen, in his late 30s, entered my office reeking of alcohol on his first appointment—not a great first impression. I thought for sure that when I looked at his charge, it would involve the word DWI or something in that realm, but Owen's charge was failure to stop and render aid. Normally, this charge would have been a felony, but somehow the case was reduced to a misdemeanor, class A. Owen's criminal record revealed two prior DWIs, and the most recent DWI probation had just been completed satisfactorily three months prior.

I asked Owen when he last consumed alcohol, and he stated he hit the bars hard last night. He knew he wouldn't be able to drink for 2 years while on probation, so he thought why not drink one last time. I asked Owen to explain the facts of his case to me.

"It was in the early wee hours of the morning in question," he began. "I have to be brutally honest, I had been drinking at a bar with some friends, we stayed till last call, and on my way home, I uh, well, I uh stopped off to, well, to be with a prostitute, and then I drove home."

"So, you remember leaving the bar, driving to another location where you were with a prostitute, and then you drove home?" I asked.

I could feel Owen was uneasy and blushing with each of my questions. His answer was yes, but not a very confident yes. Owen went on to explain that he was awakened around 2:00 pm by two San Antonio police officers. They stated that a witness identified his car as speeding around 3:45 a.m., hitting a woman with such velocity that she flew into the air and landed in the street. The officers also stated that the driver did not stop and sped away, so they were investigating.

Upon viewing the car parked in the garage, a large dent was found on the passenger-side front panel. Owen was subsequently arrested.

Smirking and nervously laughing, Owen proclaimed he had no recollection of hitting anyone or anything, stating he must have really been drunk.

The case was reduced to a misdemeanor because the prosecutor didn't have enough evidence to charge Owen with a felony. They had only one eyewitness who saw a person speeding down a poorly lit street around 3:30 in the morning, and the eyewitness couldn't tell whether the driver was a man or a woman. The investigators had a dent in Owen's car, but there was no DNA or any other evidence linking the dent to the victim. For all intents and purposes, the dent could have already been on the car when Owen allegedly hit the victim.

"My attorney was able to get me this sweet plea bargain," he told me. "The police could not put me behind the wheel of the car, so well you know."

Owen was not taking any of this very seriously. I asked him what happened to the victim, and he shrugged his shoulders and said that she died in a remorseless voice.

Owen was on probation for just a few short months. Without attaining written permission from me or the court, Owen left the state of Texas for a long weekend to attend his best friend's bachelor party in Cabo, Mexico. Owen's attorney called to inform me that Owen would not be attending his next scheduled appointment. Before hanging up, I asked if he was ok. His reply was, "He died."

In the early morning hours, Owen's body was found washed up on the resort's private beach following a night of celebration. The toxicology report revealed his blood alcohol content was that of 0.42%.

HOT SWAT

When 2:00 p.m. rolled around, it was time for a smoke break. Every Monday through Friday, rain or shine, we bitches would leave our offices to meet outside, positioning ourselves in front of the building on Doloroso. There were no benches to sit on, so we had to lean against the hot metal of the parking meters as we watched our friends who smoked light up. FYI: The Bexar County Adult Probation Department is located just one small block over from the San Antonio Police Department (SAPD). Very little, if any, conversation took place during these breaks, as we women were on a mission. You see, we are gathered together on the sidewalks of downtown San Antonio to witness the young, lean, muscular machines of the ever-so-popular San Antonio Police Department's SWAT unit.

It wouldn't be long before we would see fifteen gorgeous, tan, muscular men begin their afternoon physical training, which involves running. They would run numerous laps in front of our building before heading to the SAPD gym to lift weights and shower before their night shift began. With each new lap these gentlemen ran, they began to shed their t-shirts, using them as towels to wipe sweat from their brows as the hot sun glistened on their tan skin, revealing their calves and back muscles as they faded into the next city block.

We, women, would watch this play out for about twenty minutes before returning to our unassuming, tiny offices, feeling a warm glow in our hearts, knowing that San Antonio is just a little safer with the training and diligence of these men who were so thoughtful to grace us with their presence each workday.

Thank you, SWAT!

BITCHES AND THE BEACH

After becoming close friends at work, our next natural course of events was to travel together, so off to the beach we went. This would be the first of a gazillion trips to the Texas coast, as it was only a mere 5 hours from San Antonio. Texas is a large state with a long coastline along the Gulf. Padre Island and SPI (otherwise known as South Padre Island) are not the prettiest beaches, but they will do in a pinch. A variety of nice hotels, great restaurants, and bars, saturated with tourists for the extracurricular event of people-watching.

Let it be clear for the readers: I absolutely *hate* the beach! It's hot, with the sun blaring down, a glare coming from the ocean, and the wind whipping through your inner core. The sea breezes make it a little more bearable to endure the humid stickiness that envelopes you immediately upon entering the sand. And oh…oh that sand, it is everywhere! It creeps into your butt crack, under the boobalas, and gets inside of your bathing suit, your beach towel, and it even finds its way into the picnic lunch, no matter how carefully you pack the sandwiches. That extra crunch you get from the sand when you bite into that roast beef and brie ciabatta gourmet sandwich reminds you that eating al fresco isn't for the faint of heart when trying to enjoy your lunch on the beach. Let's not forget the throngs of people as far as the eye can see, sunbathing, flying kites, throwing footballs and frisbees, while playing loud, obnoxious music.

In my humble opinion, the beach is simply a horrific experience. In fact, the best part of going to the beach for me is being with the bitches, and that is the *only* reason I go because they all *love* it. Not to sound too magnanimous, but yes, it is a sacrifice that I am willing to make.

OH, THE THINGS WE DO FOR LOVE!

NUTS TURNS 40

Lake Travis, Austin, Texas, July: we bitches rented a condo on the lake to celebrate Nuts, who would be turning forty. Just so you know, each time we gals traveled together, alcohol was typically involved, and we have been known to get a little silly. Nothing illegal has ever transpired, and we *never, ever drink and drive*. We all loved our jobs and knew that if we were ever arrested for DWI or any other crime, we would be immediately asked to vacate the position of probation officer. So, we all practice what we preached, and we did not want to embarrass ourselves or our families, as the arrest of a probation officer most assuredly would hit the newspapers and the local six o'clock news.

On Nuts' fortieth birthday, we were in the pool, day-drinking at the place we were staying, along with other unknown holiday guests. We were positioned in the middle of the pool, holding on to a floatie, drinks in our hands, and the sun high in the midday Texas sky. Before we knew it, the sun was setting in the west, and the temperature began to get cooler as the sun burnt a bright orange, morphing into dusk. Bright stars began twinkling into the hot July evening as we bitches continued talking about our jobs, sharing the newest stories with one another.

We must have talked for hours when we all noticed that the other people in the pool had turned the music down and they had stopped talking. They were bobbing in the water near us, listening to our conversations, when a young man in his mid-30s tapped me on the shoulder.

"Excuse me, what is it that you all do for a living?" he asked.

"We're adult probation officers," I replied.

People from the wading pool to the hot tub were fixated on us, asking what seemed like a hundred questions. They wanted to know what types of people the defendants were, what crimes they committed, and whether we ever felt unsafe. What exactly does a PO do, etc.?

I know we bitches are fascinated with the type of work we do, but I didn't realize until that night in the pool how other people felt about our work and how fascinated and curious they were to hear how we spent our everyday lives with the people we surrounded ourselves with. The courthouse staff, the defense attorneys, and the defendants all contribute to our little world of criminal justice and all that it involves.

RUNNING ON EMPTY

In the late 1980s and the early 1990s, cell phones didn't exist, and although computers were in existence, they were reserved only for the stenography (steno) pool, leaving us probation officers to handwrite, using blue ink, all the defendants' reports and filing them away in filing cabinets.

Each defendant had a file, so my office was a sea of files with a desk and a chair just barely able to fit in the tiny workspace. At one point in my career, my caseload was so large that I had three file cabinets while using file boxes to house additional files. I used the file boxes as chairs for the defendant to sit on, as there was no room for furniture due to the lack of real estate in what I called an office (talk about a paper trail!). The files were organized alphabetically, making it somewhat easy to locate each defendant. With that being said, we probation officers all went through a lot of blue ink pens.

On one particular occasion, after being with the department for six months and using pens as instructed, I ran out of ink. My supervisor sent me to the steno office to get more blue pens so I could continue my work. Sounds simple enough, right? But *noooo*, not only no, but hell no. I bounced into the head steno's office and asked the simple question. "Stella, I need some blue pens. Where might I retrieve them?"

She looked up from her desk with a look I have never encountered before, her eyes glazed over, as she stood staring me down with her brown eyes and false eyelashes.

With a low and evil voice, she muttered, "Where are the pens, and are you sure they are out of ink?"

I hesitated and then replied. "Yes..sss…sss, I'm pretty sure there is no more ink in the pens," I stuttered, scared in my tracks.

Stella demanded that I go to my tiny office and bring her the dried ink pens for inspection. I slowly backed out of her office, scampering to retrieve the dry pens. Upon my return, she grabbed the two dried-up writing utensils from my hand, lit a cigarette lighter, and held the flame to the pen point. She then attempted to write with the pen on a piece of paper, and lo and behold, the pen still has life in it. I was flabbergasted and thinking to myself, "Am I on *Candid Camera*? Is this a joke? Is this lady for real?" As it turned out, she wasn't kidding. This woman was tasked with making sure we probation officers weren't getting away with squandering work supplies, including blue ink.

Let it be known far and wide across this great nation, I *never* went to Stella's office for anything throughout my stint as an officer. From that day forward, I bought my own supply of blue ink pens, hoarding them like I was saving up for the apocalypse. Even today, when I am writing with a blue pen, I can't help but chuckle and wonder, what is sweet, cheery Stella up to these days?

FROM HOARDER TO HORDING

A hoarder is an individual who compulsively collects and stores items in excess. These items are not needed and are sometimes unusual. Hoarding is also described as a form of saving, collecting, accumulating, and gathering.

I must alert you, the reader, that the information in this segment may be disturbing.

Valerie, bitch number two, had relocated with her family to Denton County, where she continued her career as an adult probation officer. We were so sad to see her go, but knew that 4 hours would not hinder our friendship. We just wouldn't be able to see her sweet face and hear her intoxicating laughter every day.

Valerie had inherited a case of a man who was on felony probation for child pornography. We will call him John. Valerie was seeing John for his scheduled appointments without incident when the Denton police department contacted her, stating that they had located a human skull in John's home. The police were interested in the skull as they thought it might be the remains of a missing person. John stated he had found the skull as a young child and had obtained it from a disturbed Indian burial site. He held onto the remains throughout his adult life.

The University of North Texas eventually was able to verify that the skull was not that of the missing person, and John's story was likely to be the truth. Valerie went to the defendant's residence with the Denton police to further investigate, and they discovered some very interesting items. The defendant, John, was present when these items were found:

*A mound of over one hundred pairs of women's underwear

*A container holding belly button lint

*A container holding fingernail clippings

Walking around the home, Valerie opened a door off the main hallway, which was the bathroom. Much to her surprise, the walls, the floor, the counter, and the sink were all covered in human feces. Valerie said that the feces had been there for a while and that there wasn't much odor emitting from the bathroom. The rest of the home was in poor condition, unkempt, and food and dirty dishes lined the kitchen counter and the sink. Valerie didn't dare open the refrigerator, leaving that for the Denton police. John's bedroom was in disarray, and the sheets looked as if they had never been introduced to a washing machine. Mounds of dirty clothes lined up on the floor, leaving a path to the bed.

As Valerie was heading out the front door of the small apartment, she noticed an item of interest. On a pony wall between the kitchen and the living room, a bluish-gray, roundish form, slightly larger than a golf ball, was poised in the middle of a flimsy paper plate. Curiously, Valerie points to the object and questions John.

"What is this?" she asked him.

Very calmly, he answered, "Oh, that, it's my sperm."

Valerie, trying to keep a cool head, replied, "OK, how did it get like this?"

"After I ejaculate, I use a hypodermic needle to form the sperm into a ball."

The item/specimen was collected and taken to a lab.

The next stop for the team was a storage unit that Valerie knew John had. With his cooperation, he had written the address and unit number on a piece of paper for them. The Denton police and Valerie located the unit and were able to pry open the door to investigate the contents. Valerie stated that the Texas heat did not disappoint that day, as it was a balmy 103 degrees when they entered the unit. For the most part, the unit was empty and didn't have anything of interest, but Valerie said she was given the gift of conjunctivitis/pink eye in both eyes from the contaminated piece of paper that John had written on.

The Denton Police Department had confiscated a computer from John's apartment, and upon reviewing the contents on that computer, they found pornographic and bestiality pornography (sexual activity between humans and animals), which ultimately would not be in John's favor. His probation was revoked, and he was sentenced to 20 years at the state penitentiary.

AFTERWORD FROM THE AUTHOR

My nearest and dearest friend, Todd, inquisitively asked me why I titled the book, "The Bitches of Bexar County?" He has known and appreciated my oddities (maybe you noticed those too throughout the book... wink) for over 40 years, and has had the pleasure of knowing the *bitches* for 35 years.

"Not one of you is a bitch," he told me. "Any one of you would give the blouse off your back, and ya'll are truly some of the kindest and wittiest women on the face of this planet."

I thusly informed Todd that, in the realm of being a probation officer, we were like s'mores. Starting from the bottom graham cracker, or the foundation of the s'more, we had to be tough, able to withstand the heaviness of the orders that were dispensed from the judges, ensuring that the defendants would carry out these orders.

Some of the defendants were granted up to 10 years of probation, so we got to know these men and women as people and were able to look beyond the crimes they had committed. This would be the marshmallow part of the s'more. When warmed up, it can be sticky, gooey, and sometimes messy. We shared in the defendant's failure, metaphorically picking them up when they failed, encouraging them to be a productive part of society. The sweet, melty chocolate part of the s'more is where we shared in their successes. Being a part of that was truly inspirational. Helping people change their lives, not just for the betterment of the defendant and their family, but also for the community in which they live.

The top layer of the s'more is the crusty, crunchy element and the toughest of all. If the defendant failed to master the rules of probation, sadly, incarceration was the next step in their story. We probation officers, for the most part, hated this step in the criminal justice system: having to stand before the judge and recommend that the defendant cannot or will not play by society's rules, resulting in their placement in prison. This ultimately takes the defendants away from their families, friends, and pets. They also miss out on birthdays, weddings, family reunions, baby christenings, graduations, and they will not be able to attend funerals to pay respect to the near and dearly departed.

On the days when I had to recommend that a defendant be sent to prison, my drive home was most assuredly not a happy one. Tears were shed as I thought of the defendants' families and friends. Their lives would forever change because their loved ones are no longer with them, be it for a short time, a long time, or a lifetime.

My life changed, too. It wasn't easy knowing that I would go about my daily routine while the defendant would face prison obstacles and challenges. The things that would happen to them are sometimes too difficult to comprehend. With each new defendant who came into my office, a little prayer was said in my head: "Please help me guide these defendants through this journey." I didn't want to bite into that imaginary s'more and not have a positive outcome.

You must have a sense of humor in this job, or you won't last. There is an enormous sense of release in being able to laugh at the atrocities we witnessed daily; it was a survival tactic. Understand, we never ever laughed *at* the defendants, but at the circumstances that led them into our world.

Let's be real, at the end of the day, we're all just people trying to make sense of it all. Striving for good health, happiness, and a safe environment where we can raise our families, be with our friends, and enjoy this crazy thing called *life*. It comes down to the choices we make and the consequences that we must all face, whether good or bad.

ABOUT THE AUTHOR

Pam Moody

Born and raised in Lubbock, Texas, Pam was brought up in a loving, Christian home. With her sister Leigh (only ten months younger) by her side, Pam describes their childhood as a *Leave It to Beaver* lifestyle. Only those old enough will remember this reference. Her father was an attorney, from whom she learned the love and respect for the law. Pam's mother was an amazing mom. She was a great listener, a tireless volunteer, tender and caring, and filled their lives with the warmth of hearth and home. She taught Pam social graces, introducing the idea of paying it forward, which then came naturally to her throughout the career choices she made. Pam's first career was as an adult probation officer, followed by her second career as a high school teacher.

After graduating from Coronado High School, Pam attended too many colleges to even name. Eventually, she graduated with a degree in psychology from Baylor University (Sic 'em Bears) in Waco, Texas (thanks to Chip and Joanna Gaines, Waco is now a city worth visiting).

Pam's life would end up along the beautiful, historical River Walk in the city of San Antonio, Texas, in Bexar County. Remember the Alamo! Her journey began here, as she entered the ominous world of criminal justice by serving as an adult probation officer for 11 years, during which she supervised defendants aged seventeen to ninety. The crimes they committed ranged from non-violent driving while their license was suspended to more violent offenses such as assaults, domestic violence, sex crimes, gang-related crimes, and murder. You name it, Pam saw it.

To Pam's surprise, she was invited to obtain her Texas teaching certification and teach eager freshmen, sophomores, juniors, and seniors at Ronald Reagan High School. She taught Criminal Justice, Principles of Law, Court Systems, Law Enforcement, and Criminal Investigations courses. For the past 25 years, Pam has been sharing the wisdom and knowledge of this most fascinating subject.

This memoir is Pam's first book. She hopes you enjoy reading it as much as she enjoyed writing it!

www.ingramcontent.com/pod-product-compliance
Lightning Source LLC
Chambersburg PA
CBHW031036160726

47991CB00005B/1898